Keep Taking the Tabloids

Fritz Spiegl was addicted to reading newspapers by the age of four, but in another country and another language. He came to England on his own as a child refugee from the Nazis, and although his musical ear helped him to pick up English quite quickly (coming top in that subject at the end of his first term at Magdalen College School) he soon found that in order to resume reading the papers he was obliged to learn a quite different form of the language. He went on to the Royal Academy of Music, while at the same time earning his living as a graphic designer, and then became First Flute in the Liverpool Philharmonic. After fifteen years he was invalided out by the decibels of the brass, but had already diversified his interests: to writing and broadcasting (both about music and words), conducting, and helping to manufacture disposable music such as TV jingles and signature tunes. He writes twice weekly for the *Liverpool Daily Post* and regularly for *The Listener*.

Fritz Spiegl

KEEP TAKING THE TABLOIDS

*What the papers say
and how they say it:*

including a News Quiz

Pan Original
Pan Books London and Sydney

First published 1983 by Pan Books Ltd,
Cavaye Place, London SW10 9PG
© Fritz Spiegl 1983
ISBN 0 330 28122 4
Photoset by Parker Typesetting Service, Leicester
Printed in Great Britain by
Richard Clay (The Chaucer Press) Ltd, Bungay, Suffolk

Contents

Author's Note

The cuttings that illustrate this book were collected over a period of more than twenty years. At first I was concerned chiefly with increasing my own understanding of what appeared to be a totally different language, but the comic and the absurd soon supervened. Then the whole thing 'snowballed' (the terminology is catching) and as I began to bore my friends with new cuttings, they in turn would draw my attention to *their* finds. Then *Private Eye*, almost as soon as it came into being, started to draw on my collection (and Richard Ingrams chose to call them 'Fritz's Spiegels' – the misspelling intentional), which further widened the catchment area as the paper's own readers began to send me cuttings. Meanwhile I had already published three of my own little books (*What the Papers Didn't Mean to Say*, etc.) with the Scouse Press of Liverpool; but I have also CLAWED BACK←* some of my old *Private Eye* material. Thus the contents of this book are based on what is probably the biggest collection of its kind.

It should be added that some of the cuttings have had to be reconstituted because of the quick deterioration of newsprint and so as to avoid one or two distracting details such as pre-decimal coinage, etc. This has had the incidental result of simplifying the copyright of my book: naturally, I am not prepared to reveal which cuttings are original and which remade – for this makes it easier to stop those notorious scavengers, the quizmasters of radio panel games and chat-show entertainers in search of a quick second-hand joke: they first raid other men's books and then re-anthologise the spoils as their own. I hereby 'spell out' a warning 'loud and clear'. As regards provenance of my illustrations, it was decided that a tactful silence would be preferred to my giving attributions. It is all meant in good part.

Among the many friends to whom I am grateful for help and encouragement are: Fred Adler, John Amis, Kingsley Amis, William Amos, Dr Eleanor Ashton, Tony Austin, Jim Black, Alan Brack, Sheila Britten, Reg Brookes, Moran Caplat, Geoffrey Churney, George Glover, Dr Myer Goldman, Barrie Hall, Gillian Hush, Barrie Iliffe, Jennifer Kale, Joanne Keane, M. R. Kilduff, Beresford King-Smith, Jim Mansell, Graham Melville-Mason, Rachael Orme, Iain M. Paterson, Steve Race, Bill Smithies, Peter Spaull, Dr Jackie Stedmon, Peter Stroud, Mike Sumner, David Stuckey, Philip Towell, Michael Unger, Meirion Williams, Hugh Wood.

Special thanks are due to Mrs Dorothy Stanton for constant encouragement, and above all to my wife Ingrid, who helped ceaselessly. We must be the only couple in the world who communicate at breakfast through holes cut in newspapers.

*The use of small capital letters plus the arrow symbol indicates throughout that the word or phrase in question may be found in An A-Z of English News-write which begins on page 56.

Introduction: Some Notes on the Changing Styles of Newspaper English

In about 1880 the chemist and patent-medicine manufacturer Sir Henry Wellcome invented a new medicinal tablet. Until then, Victorian patients had had to take their medicine either by powder in a draught or in big tablets such as are now known as 'horse-pills'. Wellcome put on the market a more palatable and highly compressed pill. He named his invention 'tabloid' (combining the first syllable of 'tablet' with the Greek suffix -*oid*, denoting likeness) and on 14 March 1884 registered the word as the property of his firm, Burroughs, Wellcome & Company Ltd. The tabloid was an instant success. Not only did the trade-name enter the popular language but in due course the word came to be applied to anything minature, or that was smaller than expected, not unlike the more recent vogue-prefix 'mini' (which, incidentally, was also a registered trade-name – belonging to Eavestaff's Minipiano long before the advent of the Mini car or mini-skirt). For example, when Sir Thomas Sopwith built a small and highly agile fighter-plane at the beginning of the First World War he named it the Sopwith Tabloid.

It was not until about 1925 that the newspaper magnate Lord North-cliffe proposed the establishment of what he informally described in a speech as a 'tabloid newspaper', much as he might today have spoken of a 'mini-newspaper'. He was referring only to its size, not the style in which it was written. For when the first tabloid newspapers eventually arrived, their language was still much the same as that of the broadsheets; that is, leaning towards the long-winded, verbose and over-inflated prose of Victorian penny-a-line journalism. The fact that modern tabloids were later to present news in a highly compressed form, easily swallowed and quickly assimilated, did not enter Lord Northcliffe's head.

There is nothing so old-fashioned as an old newspaper. Whenever we find a copy five, ten or twenty years old, we are struck by great differences – in layout, in the way the headlines are arranged, in typefaces, picture captions and, provided one goes back far enough, in prose style. Until about 1900 there were no illustrations, or at any rate photographic ones, for dot-screen photo-engraved halftone reproduction lagged behind the invention of photography by about half a century. Thus a full page of *The Times* would have no pictures, few headlines and no displayed type. What headlines there were would be hardly bigger than the capital letters of the body type. The more popular papers printed bigger headlines, arranged in 'decks' and in a variety of type-styles. These multi-deckers would serve to inform the reader by skilful summary, and so let him decide at a glance whether he wanted to read the full story or pass on to another.

Most serious foreign newspapers have retained the factual, non-sensational multi-decker headline which English ones appear to have all but abandoned: French, German, Dutch and Scandinavian papers (even American ones, and they invented sensational journalism) give their readers informative headlines of moderate size that reflect the content of the text they surmount.

But English headline style has in the last decade changed to an extraordinary degree. Instead of quietly informing the reader, headlines now either tease with shouted riddles, or try to amuse – and more likely annoy – him with predictable puns and worn-out clichés that are repeated day after day. Or else produce ambiguous nonsense. The three national 'quality' papers and the Sunday 'heavies' (as well as one or two provincials) are only slightly less blatant about it than the tabloids; and the constant movement of employees between newspapers helps gradually to extinguish differences in house-style. The difference in headline style in particular is getting smaller all the time. There was a public argument a year or two ago as to whether the headline pun was invented by the *Guardian* or *Daily Mirror*.

Rubber weakens in the squeeze

NEW SHIP DESIGN MAY SAVE YARDS

Dingo mother's baby taken away

Judge lifts board ban on woman

U.S. Loses Its Grip on British Lard Market

Weinstock blackball row snowballs

RANDMOTHER Mrs Evelyn ones yesterday won a court attle against an insurance mpany, which stopped her ining its "board of delegates" because she was a woman.

RATS CLOSE SCHOOL

An invasion of rats and fleas closed Checkley Memorial School near Tean, Staffs, yesterday, while contractors fumigated the building.

SURGEONS SEW BACK LEG OF SIX-YEAR-OLD

Stocks cushion butter rise

By Our Belfast Correspondent

Surgeons at a Northern Ireland hospital have sewn back the rig of a six-year-old y af severed below a tractor epublic.

TROOPS SENT TO MASSACRE VILLAGES

Troop reinfor been rushed to where hundreds includ

COMPREHENSIVE MISTRESS IS STABBED

A 24-year-old woman teac. was stabbed in the back with a five-inch dagger in a school

SEVERED FEET FACTORY TO FACE CHARGES

The firm involved in the acci- ent in which a youth had his et severed, is to be taken to

Such brevity, far from being the soul of wit, is even the death of meaning.

G. K. CHESTERTON

For real, old-fashioned design and informative English free from facetious puns and tedious clichés one must go to the *International Herald Tribune* or one of the smaller Irish newspapers. Even some of the English-language African newspapers, in spite of occasional lapses, preserve much of the former dignity of Fleet Street style.

As regards modern newspaper prose there is a certain parallel between tabloid English and Greek, that universal fount of all that is beautiful in most European languages. Greek takes several forms: classical and New Testament Greek, which have as little to do with *dhimotiki* (the name for the everyday, colloquial speech one might use for ordering one's mousaka or taramosalata) as Chaucer or Shakespeare have with modern, conversational English. And there is *katharevousa*, which is used in newspapers – a stilted, formal Greek that would be totally unintelligible to the shepherd on the hills. It produced a kind of journalistic élitism which many people deplored; and in fact recent political trends have led to a more demotic form of newspaper writing, understood by ordinary readers.

Although current newspaper English holds no secrets for anyone familiar with English speech, it, too, makes use of a stilted and formal language which has a curiously mock-archaic flavour, full of words and phrases that are never heard in ordinary everyday speech. Unlike the facetious headline (which probably tries to compete with the breezy, fast-talking and generally excruciating spoken English of junk-radio disc jockeys) newspaper *prose*, the language in which the stories themselves are presented, looks backwards to a forgotten age and forgotten styles. The construction of sentences is often mannered to an absurd degree, with all kinds of artificial inversions and a vocabulary that went out of ordinary speech with the First World War. The choice of words is limited – reflecting, no doubt, the haste with which papers are produced – and the general effect is nearly always totally predictable and sometimes downright foolish. In this respect some papers are worse than others and there is, of course, a great difference in style between a leading article (now more often known by its American name, editorial) in *The Times*, the *Guardian* or the *Daily Telegraph* on the one hand, and the *Mirror* or *Daily Star* on the other. Features pages, too, may reflect a more considered approach, for they are usually made up a day or two ahead. Some of the tabloids' writers refuse to believe that their readers can digest more than a few words at a time. They therefore make sentences short. To the point. Often verbless. Staccato. And ugly. As John Aubrey wrote about a classical author: 'Seneca writes as a Boare does pisse, [namely] by jirkes.'

It is for the hard news that the ready-made phrase comes into its own. Words, phrases, whole sentences even, appear to be mass-produced like plastic kitchen-utensils, each one identical to the next. It is a language of its own, never encountered in real life. Even the most hardened news reporter abandons it as he leaves the office. If he did not, here is how he might converse with his wife (doubtless 'common law' and also a journalist) at the breakfast table.

That was postman Fred Rigg riding high on his bike, peddling his mailbag. He brought a letter from Mum, shapely blonde vivacious divorcee, mother of six, Rita Grunge (58), which has just landed on the doormat with a sickening thud. It's ages since she's been to see us. Says she wants to take a stroll down memory lane. I can see from your face that you're pleased. The smile that says it all!

So a visit from battling granny is looming, is it? I suppose she's adamant. Fancy dropping that bombshell on us at this moment in time.

Yes, and I'm afraid there's more shock horror in store. She wants to bring boyfriend, portly bowlerhatted bespectacled retired bricklayer Ron Glubb (72). He still seems to be a reluctant groom, unwilling to pop the question. I have a gut reaction feeling he doesn't want to be wed to her. At first her hopes rose, then they faded and now seem dashed. He's probably thinking in terms of remaining an office romeo.

Yes, and she his common-law wife.

Looks like their whirlwind courtship's come to nothing. Anyway, you know I can't stand him. We'll have eyeball-to-eyeball confrontation situations all weekend. It's potential dynamite. Besides, he'll be quaffing all my scotch and puffing my giant havanas.

Well, it's odds-on he hasn't got his pensioner's rail-card in time and so won't be able to make tracks. Just the ticket! But he vowed he'd try. Meanwhile we're walking a tightrope.

How's Mum then?

Oh, alive and well and living in Manchester's Didsbury.

Well, tell them not to bring the cat. Whenever it sees the budgie . . .

Yes, I know. The fur and feathers fly.

Darling, you read my mind. Just purrfect, you are!

So the trip's balanced on a knife-edge, is it?

Well, when they came last Christmas it was a bit of a nightmare dash for them, and Easter was a carbon copy. It's becoming an ongoing saga. Why don't they fly out of London's Airport into Majorca? But I suppose we'll have to give them the green light.

Look! Darren (2), is making a bid to grab the pinta. If he's not careful it'll hurtle to the floor and he'll plummet after it. Why can't the boy tuck into his cornflakes 'n' milk? Yesterday he tripped over his shoelace and plunged headlong to the floor. Came down to earth with a bump, he did. He's just dicing with death, that child. Really, he'll have to munch breakfast amid tight security.

Darren! Be a good boy and tuck into your breakfast. I sometimes feel I could slay that babe-in-arms. I've spelt out a warning to him over it, *loud and clear. In another month or two he'll be so spoilt he'll think he's got a toddlers' charter, a licence to . . . And he's got egg on his face. Why don't you whisk him to the bathroom? You might probe his nappy at the same time – and put his potty under him – strategically placed.*

Don't sound so shell-shocked. After all, he's our only love-child.

Old enough to get a tongue-lashing over it. When I was little I was so naughty I used to wander off. One time a fair cop brought me back in her panda car. Now he's losing his nappy! I can see all the bare facts. A big cover-up is called for.

Oh, I'm out of smokes. D'you think you could make a mercy dash to the corner shop and get me some of those famed filter-tips as seen on TV?

Yes. I've got to go buy a couple of chops from 47-year-old jovial bachelor, singing butcher Ted Jones. He's been hitting the high notes at last and is to sing in Nottingham's Town Hall next week. His prices have really soared recently, so I thought I'd give him the chop. Which reminds me. I've got no cash.

Well, call in at the friendly neighbourhood High Street bank and get some crisp oncers. And don't drag your feet.

Last time I went, it was a nightmare visit. The manager said we were overdrawn and spelled out a warning, loud and clear. Red faces! It was a body blow, I can tell you. And anyway, how many times have I underlined to you that smoking may damage your health? Only last week the Minister of Health slammed it. This is one matter over which we're always on a collision course.

Yes, we're split over it right down the middle.

If news prose changes slowly, it is, paradoxically, because it is always compiled in haste: the hard-pressed journalist finds it quicker to select some old, well-worn cliché from the jargon repertoire of his trade than to invent a bright new one (and even if he does, his colleagues may despise him for being a smart alec: it is significant that the very word 'cliché' is a French newspaper and printing term, also used in German as *Klischee*, for a printing-plate or block that can be re-used over and over again). That is why we read in our papers today outmoded and stiltedly archaic phrases about 'mothballs', 'carbon copies', 'blueprints' or 'milestones' (when did you last rely on a milestone for roadside information?); about people who do not retire but 'bow out' (presumably walking backwards with a low, courtly obeisance and a sweep of their wide-brimmed hat); about 'adamant' people who may be 'tightlipped and ashenfaced', but, like cows, 'munch' their meals (generally 'slap-up' ones), and 'quaff' their drink noisily like Falstaff. People who take risks alliteratively 'dice with death'; police never make a simple arrest but 'swoop' or 'pounce' (except in the *Guardian*, the delightful pioneer of the Black-on-White Misprint Show, where they once inadvertently 'ponced'). Policemen always look for someone able to 'help with their enquiries'. There is no fire, however small, that cannot be elevated into a 'blaze'; or, if a corpse is found, the result of 'suspected foul play' ('*play*'?), they search not for a killer but a 'slayer'. The archaic word 'slay' was in the first place probably revived for its convenient brevity as a headline word. It is no shorter than 'kill', but has a supposedly dramatic ring that goes back to the erring sons of Adam. Seven decades after the First World War, people still 'take the flak', are 'strafed', and suffer from 'shell-shock', though this now afflicts only housewives when the price of eggs rises; or rather, 'soars'. A century after Zola's famous *J'accuse* (an arresting headline if ever there was one) we still 'Name these guilty men!' But headline words soon make their way into body-matter, which is the name for the smaller print of the text. There you will seldom find words that are left lonely and on their own ('out in the cold'?): they all have their inseparable, faithful mates, making every denial 'categorical', every battle 'pitched', all Christians 'committed' and homosexuals 'practising'; banknotes are always 'crisp'; and not a pair of ordinary, or even weak, binoculars is to be had: they are never less than 'powerful'. No musical story is ever reported without automatic recourse to 'notes'. These are 'struck' or 'hit' and, according to context, may be 'high' or 'low', 'discordant' or 'sour'. Hopes either 'rise', 'fade' or are 'dashed'.

The Fleet Street Ages of Man

The Ages of Man as seen by Fleet Street may begin with a 'miracle baby', which becomes a 'babe-in-arms', grows into a 'toddler', 'tot', and then a 'kid'. If his parents are divorced and disputing custody, he may turn into a 'tug-of-love' baby, toddler or kid – with horrific suggestions of two people tearing out his arms as in a tug-of-war. Schoolchildren are sometimes described as school 'students', especially in the left-wing and sociological press (they have even been encouraged to form their own mini-militant union, the National Union of School Students), while still 'teenagers'. Girl teenagers who become pregnant are 'gymslip mums' when they are still at school, but mere 'mums-to-be' as soon as they have left, even at the age of fifteen and still wearing their gymslips. An illegitimate baby is a 'love-child', and the place in which it is thought to have been produced, a 'love-nest' – for love is apparently thought never to enter into married relationships. A 'boy' becomes a 'youth' at about sixteen and a man at nineteen; but he may remain a 'boy-friend' even into his seventies. Women can be called 'girls' into their mid-thirties and 'girl-friends' up to any age. When actors, actresses or ballet dancers are the subject of a story they remain 'boys' and 'girls' for ever. There are also compound terms which can be made into almost any permutation, such as 'teenage fathers', 'gymslip muggers' or 'singing bachelor', etc.

The subject's marital or professional status ('bachelor', 'businessman', 'housewife', 'divorcee'), his or her age, whether germane to the story or not – and, if a woman, her hair colour, breast, waist and hip measurements and some indication of her attractiveness, with carefully graded euphemisms ('blonde, vivacious have-a-go housewife, Eileen Grunge, 38, 44, 49') – are considered essential information. So are the existence and number of children, if any; and even the knowledge that the subject's children have proved their own fertility ('battling grandfather of four, Bert Snodgrass, 73'). But from the age of sixty to sixty-five Fleet Street Man's decline is rapid – into plain pensioner, *sans* teeth, *sans* dignity, *sans* everything.

Bogus Titles, Phoney Professions and Missing Articles

Apparently unconnected facts are strung together and piled up in front of a person's name, with the invariable omission of the definite or indefinite article: 'Missing murder suspect Lord Lucan', 'Squandering heiress Pamela Kleyff', 'Hole-in-heart boy John Barker', 'Wife-swapping cowman Alfred Smith', 'Whooping-cough vaccine victim Kevin Capper', 'Retching Oliver Reed' . . . in an inelegant procession of bogus titles and spurious professions – all awarded by pressmen too much in a hurry (or too lazy) to rewrite the information they receive from a teleprinter. For that is how this foolish practice has come about. In America, where it originated, the style is sometimes called 'Morkrumbo', a portmanteau word made from 'Morkrum' + 'mumbo-jumbo', the former being the trade name of a kind of teleprinter. It is of course a sensible and legitimate practice, when copy is being transmitted by cable or teleprinter (and now computer print-out), to cram all available information as close as possible to the subject's name. We owe its spread into news prose to *Time* magazine, whose wide British circulation had considerable influence on British journalists from the late 1940s onwards.

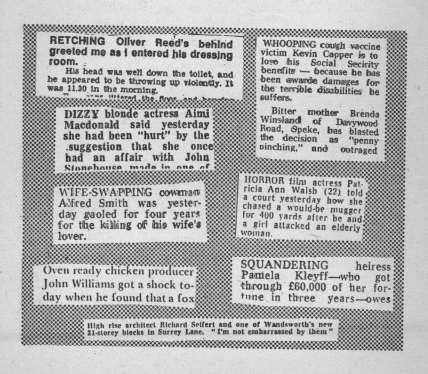

RETCHING Oliver Reed's behind greeted me as I entered his dressing room.

His head was well down the toilet, and he appeared to be throwing up violently. It was 11.30 in the morning.

DIZZY blonde actress Aimi Macdonald said yesterday she had been "hurt" by the suggestion that she once had an affair with John Stonehouse made in one of

WIFE-SWAPPING cowman Alfred Smith was yesterday gaoled for four years for the killing of his wife's lover.

Oven ready chicken producer John Williams got a shock today when he found that a fox

WHOOPING cough vaccine victim Kevin Capper is to lose his Social Security benefits — because he has been awarde damages for the terrible disabilities he suffers.

Bitter mother Brenda Winsland of Davywood Road, Speke, has blasted the decision as "penny pinching," and outraged

HORROR film actress Patricia Ann Walsh (22) told a court yesterday how she chased a would-be mugger for 400 yards after he and a girl attacked an elderly woman.

SQUANDERING heiress Pamela Kleyff—who got through £60,000 of her fortune in three years—owes

High rise architect Richard Seifert and one of Wandsworth's new 21-storey blocks in Surrey Lane. "I'm not embarrassed by them"

Green monkey disease victim Geoffrey Platt is continuing to make a slow improvement in his airtight plastic tent at the Coppett's

SUSPECTED urban guerrilla, Mr Uwe Folkerts, will go on trial in Stuttgart on August 17 for membership of a criminal organisation, the state

TEACHER Miss Tania Szabo (above), 37-year-old daughter of war heroine Violette Szabo, was congratulated at London

Hole-in-the-heart boy John Barker, aged two, could become another of Liverpool's homeless by Friday.

Her husband, Scot James Henderson, lifted the veil of misery which had shrouded her life for four years—ever since she was

One of the first to greet him was fellow George Davis campaigner, Young Liberal leader Mr Peter Hain.

Reconditioned Piano Specialist Mrs. Gordon's prices are drastically reduced until February 2nd with some spectacular bargains this

PEDALLING pensioners Bert and Queenie Barnes rode home yesterday after a 5,000-mile trip across America. Bert (69), and Queenie (64), crossed the continent on their bikes from Los Angeles to New York in 14 weeks, sleeping in a tent. Adventures included a brush with a mountain lion and a camp fire meal with cowboys on a cattle drive.

Soaring cost of death sentence wife's case

Axe attack whip wife freed

Mourners pack bone marrow boy's funeral

BONE BOY MOTHER FIGHTS ON

Names and Nicknames

Apart from the bogus titles and descriptive pile-ups (see above) used in order to save time (and a definite or indefinite article), newspapers also like to give people nicknames. These may be simple abbreviations like Maggie, Ted, Shirl, Jim or Willie for ministers of the crown, given them not out of affectionate informality but to save headline space. It is noteworthy that such nicknames are not applied to all notable politicians. Sir Harold Wilson was never 'Harry', and Sir Alec Douglas Home neither 'Alec' nor 'Douggie'. Publicity agents' inventions – like 'Joe (Mr Piano) Henderson' or 'The Man with the Golden Flute' – are blindly copied. So are nicknames originally given to children in the cradle or by comrades in the armed services, if newsmen can get hold of them; and these are then applied to adults with monotonous and often incongruous regularity: there was a time when a particular soldier-adventurer was much in the news, and readers were given the impression that many years previously a priest had said, 'I name this child Mad Mike.' But *The Times* tends to err on the side of excessive formality. Even if some trade union leader or pop musician prefers to be known as Joe Soap, Bill Keyes or Len Murray (as trade union leaders and pop musicians generally do), that paper will call them Mr Joseph Soap, Mr William Keyes and Mr Lionel Murray, respectively. On one occasion it recorded the birthday of a Mr David Brubeck.

There are also sinister and often exaggerated sobriquets, some of them copied from the criminal underworld and used in the papers for their sensation value: Big H, the Mad Axeman, Henry the Greek, the Black Panther, Yorkshire Ripper, etc. When some gangsters near-murdered a train-driver (who subsequently died) and stole a lot of money, the crime became known as the Great Train Robbery. Fleet Street then transferred the name to the gangsters, calling them 'Great Train Robbers', thus appearing to thrust greatness upon them. The leader of a gang may become Mr Big, and a politician not known for taking bribes, Mr Clean. (The latter is American, taken from the name of a patent household cleanser familiar in every home.)

Inanimate things also get nicknames, like the BLACK BOX← and the SPY IN THE CAB←. It could be argued that if the latter had been allowed to keep its non-emotive name 'tachograph' it might have been accepted sooner by the British lorry-driver. One of the most extraordinary and tasteless nicknames was given in the early 1980s, when a woman from the county of Avon was murdered. Most newspapers referred to her as 'the Avon Lady' – the name of house-to-house cosmetics saleswomen and of a race-horse.

RU to relax rules on BARLA

Ministry to hold talks on D-notice review

AA BACKS B-TEST DRIVE

Two new suspected F and M cases

L-DRIVER FAILED 4 B-TESTS

Cyclists in N-protest marathon

Avon husband will riddle

N-shelter planned for city

WHO in fight for vaccine

THE FAMILY of missing Avon lady Linda Sturley pledged last night to fight her husband's will to keep his mistress out of it.

T-Line suspended

'Mr Clean' named by Reagan

'Big H' arrested

POLICE NAME MR. BIG

The Geographical Possessive

One of the quirks of English is that the possessive goes well only with what is animate: 'the man's gun, the child's table, the dog's foot' – but not 'the gun's barrel' or 'the table's leg'. Thus, 'Liverpool's captain' looks and sounds right when a sports team is meant, but 'Liverpool's Lime Street Station' is not only ugly but a waste of an apostrophe: 'gun barrel' and 'Liverpool Lime Street' are better and simpler English. Like Bogus Titles, the Geographical Possessive comes from the teleprinter. Where a writer would put 'I walked down Oxford Street in London', the hack instinctively walks down 'London's Oxford Street.'

The Knee-jerk Pun – Snow Joke!

There is nothing so predictable and inevitable as the newspaper pun – more predictable even than the seasons. Every summer, as the temperatures 'soar' (for they never simply rise), 'Phew what a scorcher!' appears on the tabloid front pages, occasionally relieved by more factual inevitabilities like '84 and still rising!' As winter comes ('the whole country in its icy grip'), 'It's snow joke', and someone, somewhere is bound to be 'dreaming of a white Christmas' – that is, if snow is 'on the cards'. Or it's simply 'BRR!'

Has there ever been a winning animal in a cat or dog show that has not been described as 'top cat' or 'top dog', with, in the case of the former, a 'purrfect!' somewhere in the picture caption?

Making tracks for age of the cycle

Bitter side of pub business

Butcher leaves bobbies facing a roasting

A COWBOY butcher has rustled up some red faces among the boys in blue at a Liverpool police station.

The cheeky trader called at St Annes Street station, offering cut-price meat to the bobbies just before Christmas.

Now it has been revealed that the butcher is on the police wanted list for being a rustler, and some officers could be in for a roasting.

Bicycle rack
Brenda Polan freewheels into fashion.

GRIMSBY FISHERMAN NETS FIRST PRIZE

FRANK HARTLEY (34), the young singing fisherman who last year thought he would never sing again, has won the 1st

SURE FIRE CURE FOR DRINK

By CHRISTOPHER MUNNION
in Johannesburg

A WOMAN in South Africa cured her husband of his drinking problem when she emptied a pistol in his direction wounding him twice

Army ads get the bullet

The cost of living changes frequently enough to bring its own obligatory descriptions. Bacon prices are 'sliced', house prices 'go through the roof' – and it's a 'black day for coalmen'. The declining habit of cigarette smoking leaves 'tobacconists fuming'. Beer price rises are a 'bitter blow' to drinkers – though there is occasionally a 'mild' side to the publican's business.

Transport gets a 'rough ride'. Cyclists either 'ride high' (how?) or 'fall flat', their aspirations 'punctured'. Trains are 'on the right tracks' or else 'off the rails'. Ships 'sail high' (how?) or into 'troubled waters'. But when things maritime or naval are not going too well, they are 'depth-charged', 'torpedoed' or simply 'sunk'.

The army 'gets the bullet' and the announcement of defence cuts drops a bombshell' (how?). Anything to do with guns is either 'surefire' or 'off target'.

Golfers are 'stymied', snooker players 'on cue', riders of horses 'come a cropper', cricketers may be 'stumped' even when they are a thousand miles away from the nearest wicket.

Cycle boom goes flat

THE BICYCLE boom in over and British manufacturers are having to do a lot of back-pedalling to cut production costs.

ON CUE FOR £3,000 CLAIM

Just over a year ago the industry was riding high. Cycling became a craze. More and more people took heed of health

Daily Telegraph Reporter

BILL WERBENIUK may only be ranked 9th in the world of snooker but he became the envy of

White Christmas is on the cards

Tobacconists fuming

It is all very harmless but inexpressibly silly, especially as English is a language second to none (except possibly French) for clever, punning and witty word-play. The desperate search for a feeble pun may even cause offence. The *Guardian*, which during the 1960s pioneered the headline pun (apart from a few even feebler attempts occasionally seen earlier in the *Daily Mirror*), at one time almost made a habit of printing news about the Chinese under the headline 'Chinks in the Bamboo Curtain' – until one of its own contributors felt obliged to write to the paper explaining that he was not responsible for the headline which surmounted his (very serious) article. But it is perhaps not surprising to find that among non-Caucasian people only the Chinese and Japanese (e.g. 'A nip in the air' as a caption for a photograph of a Japanese plane) become the butt of race jokes. You will search in vain for the words 'black' or 'coloured' being used in a joke context (except by accident); and mere mention of the proverbial 'nigger in the woodpile' would bring the whole weight of the race relations industry down on the offender like the equally proverbial but not proscribed 'ton of bricks'. The *Guardian* for some inexplicable reason has taken to totally meaningless headline puns that are not puns at all but simply misspellings: 'torque' for 'talk', 'rap' for 'wrap', 'rite' for 'right', 'vain' for 'vane' etc. Underlying this may be a genuine uncertainty about the spelling in the required context. The comedian Marty Feldman would probably have been amused had he known that his obituary would appear under the punning headline 'Beau jester'; after all, he did make a film of *Beau Geste*. But 'Hot under the cholera' for a harrowing report about an epidemic can only be described as the worst of bad taste.

Marty Feldman

Hot under the cholera

Beau jester

Acid drops

HYDROCHLORIC acid has been discovered in eye drops on sale in Colorado, less than two weeks after seven people died in the Chicago area from taking headache pills containing cyanide.

Heaven scent

Fourth bridge

Guilt edged

Pattern of tiny feet

Role call

Myth and hit

Joyce items

Fertility right

Gift rap

WEATHER VAIN

Excuse me pleas

Polly gone

Shop flaw

Clube root

Sir,—Alan Pickup writes with apparent awe at the audacity of Drs Napier and Clube, in suggesting that

People who have names like Smellie or ending with '-cock' or '-bottom' get used from their schooldays onwards to having jokes made on their surname; they learn simply to ignore every jokester (each of whom thinks he is the first to hit on the idea) with an inward curse and a resigned expression. None of this worries our headline writers. They, too, think they have had 'this absolutely *brilliant* idea . . .' for the very first time.

I can imagine the following conversation taking place in Shoe Lane or Farringdon Road one weekday night at about eleven.

First Sub-editor: Here's a report from Honduras. Seems a church spire collapsed while the choirboys were tolling the bell for evensong. The priest apparently spanked one of them for being naughty, so he climbed up and loosened a rafter. Nineteen killed and 30 injured. How about HEAVY TOLL, eh? (Wipes tears of mirth from his eyes).

Second Sub: No, better make it TOLLED OFF. And here's a good one. 'The death is announced of Sir Ernest . . .'

First Sub: Stop, Charles. I know what you're going to say. (Both together): DEAD ERNEST! Hang on. Better see what the Editor thinks about it.

A minute later, returns, fingering a large bump on his head: He hit me. The dirty rotten sod. He hit me, Nigel. He said: 'Take this load of rubbish away' — and then he thumped me on the head with a ruler.

Second Sub: He was quite right. Nigel. Only doing his job. After all, he's the 'EAD ITTER, isn't he?

First Sub: I don't think that's at all funny, Charles.

The Stately Homes of England (and other Song and Book Titles)

'Stately home' was popularised as a cliché expression by a song from Noël Coward's show *Operetta*, first produced at His Majesty's Theatre, London, in 1938:

The Stately Homes of England,
How beautiful they stand,
To prove the Upper Classes
Have still the Upper Hand

But Coward himself was merely parodying a once popular ballad by Felicia Dorothea Hemans (1793–1835), the Liverpool poetess (as she called herself in those far-off, pre-liberation days):

The stately homes of England,
How beautiful they stand!
Amidst their tall, ancestral trees,
O'er all the pleasant land.

Mrs Hemans gave us another much-quoted line: 'The boy stood on the burning deck'; but when it comes to song-titles-turned-clichés, Coward is an easy winner: 'Poor Little Rich Girl', 'A Room with a View', 'Don't Put your Daughter on the Stage, Mrs Worthington', 'Don't let's be beastly to the Germans', 'Chase me, Charlie', etc.

ANATOMY Some stock newspaper phrases go back to more distant times. Robert Burton (1577–1640) used the word 'anatomy' effectively, aptly and in an entirely original manner in the title of his book *The Anatomy of Melancholy* (1621). From then until the middle of the twentieth century the word kept its anatomical, medical associations, with various digressions in shades of meaning: for example, 'an anatomy' was the popular name for an articulated skeleton used in the teaching of medicine and surgery (*Anatome* is the Greek word for dissection, from *ana* = up, + *tome*, a cutting.) But then, in 1965, Anthony Sampson published the first of a series of books analysing the state of Britain, each with a title beginning *The Anatomy of . . .* – and thereafter the word became irresistible to the media parrots. Sampson published a further *Anatomy* in 1982.

COMING IN FROM THE COLD is derived from the book by John le Carré, *The Spy who Came in from the Cold* (1963), and when used as an often-recurring press cliché refers to someone, not necessarily a spy, who returns to favour or to his former way of life, perhaps after a period of inaction or loss of office. Those who fail to 'come in from the cold' are usually said to be 'left out' in it.

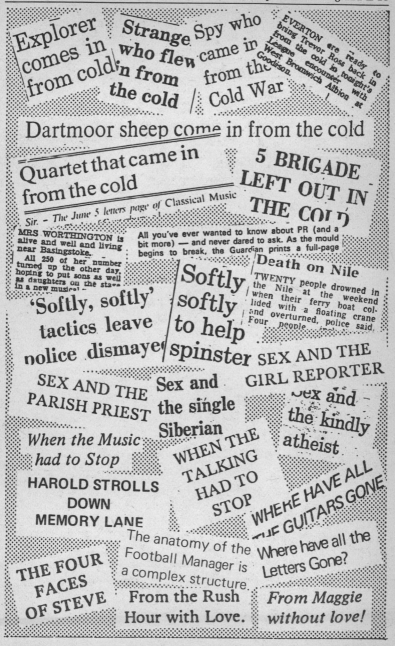

Explorer comes in from cold

Strange Spy who who flew came in 'n from from the the cold Cold War

EVERTON are ready to bring Trevor Ross back in from the cold in tonight's League encounter with West Bromwich Albion at Goodison.

Dartmoor sheep come in from the cold

Quartet that came in from the cold

5 BRIGADE LEFT OUT IN THE COLD

Sir. – The June 5 letters page of Classical Music

MRS WORTHINGTON is alive and well and living near Basingstoke.
All 250 of her number turned up the other day, hoping to put sons as well as daughters on the stage in a new musical –

All you've ever wanted to know about PR (and a bit more) — and never dared to ask. As the mould begins to break, the Guardian prints a full-page

'Softly, softly' tactics leave police dismayed

Softly softly to help spinster

Death on Nile

TWENTY people drowned in the Nile at the weekend when their ferry boat collided with a floating crane and overturned, police said. Four people

SEX AND THE PARISH PRIEST

Sex and the single Siberian

SEX AND THE GIRL REPORTER

Sex and the kindly atheist

When the Music had to Stop

WHEN THE TALKING HAD TO STOP

HAROLD STROLLS DOWN MEMORY LANE

WHERE HAVE ALL THE GUITARS GONE

The anatomy of the Football Manager is a complex structure.

Where have all the Letters Gone?

THE FOUR FACES OF STEVE

From the Rush Hour with Love.

From Maggie without love!

EVERYTHING (ALL) YOU EVER WANTED TO KNOW comes from a book and film title, *Everything You Always Wanted to Know About Sex but Never Dared Ask*. The adoption of such a clumsy title into newspaper cliché language is more a tribute to the success of the book than to the originality of journalists.

FINGERLICKIN' GOOD, meaning good to eat, pleasant-tasting, comes from an advertisement for fried chicken featuring an elderly man (who bore the self-awarded rank of colonel) unhygenically licking his fingers while serving his customers with food – a disgusting habit that should be discouraged among catering workers. 'Colonel' Sanders is now dead and, although Kentucky Fried Chicken is still eaten, the posters seem to have disappeared. But the phrase lives on.

THE FOUR FACES OF . . . From a book and film entitled *The Four Faces of Eve*, a schizophrenic. When the title is used as a news phrase, the number of faces is variable.

FROM (RUSSIA) WITH (LOVE) . . . From a book by Ian Fleming (1957).

MEMORY LANE An unadopted road found in every newspaper's collection of mythical street names. People are said to take a walk, stroll or trip down memory lane when they revisit old haunts; or merely revive memories without stirring from their armchairs, perhaps by listening to old gramophone records. It is also a favourite picture-caption cliché. Its origin probably lies in a popular hit record of the 1920s and 1930s, 'Down Memory Lane', by De Silva.

SEX AND . . . Stock headline derived from a book by Helen Gourlay Brown, entitled *Sex and the Single Girl*.

SOFTLY SOFTLY From a saying once common among British soldiers and sailors, 'Softly, softly catchee monkey', which they probably attributed to Confucius. It has now been completely absorbed into English jargon, and statements such as 'We favour the softly softly approach to this problem . . .' are made in all seriousness and without self-consciousness even by ministers of the crown. The phrase is used to describe a gradual plan or process.

WHEN THE . . . HAD TO STOP From the poem by Robert Browning, *A Toccata of Galuppi's* –

What of soul was left, I wonder,
When the kissing had to stop?

The second line of this couplet was used in 1960 as the title of a book by Constantine Fitzgibbon and subsequently done to death in many combinations and applications.

WHERE HAVE ALL THE . . . GONE? From a modern, commercial 'folk' song by P. Seeger, in which he deplores by means of reiterated platitudes the alleged disappearance of flowers. The song enjoyed some popularity in the 1960s, especially as a kind of theme song of militant peace protesters, and sounds even more mawkish when intoned in the tuneless speech-song of Marlene Dietrich as 'Sag mir wo die Blumen sind', or in French as 'Que sont devenues les fleurs?' But worst of all is its frequent use as a boring headline cliché.

Carefully Orchestrated – in a Wrong Key

The press and politicians have an unerring instinct for appropriating the jargon of the professions – and then misusing it. With a 'concerted effort' they 'jump on the musicians' bandwagon', 'pull out all the stops' with much 'brio', and 'carefully orchestrate' their 'recurring leitmotif' in a 'low key'. This can be 'offbeat', 'upbeat' or 'downbeat', or merely a 'dull ostinato counterpoint', but the 'keynote' of their 'organs' is always to resist any 'offkey soft-pedalling' in spite of a 'discordantly staccato chorus of disapproval'. When necessary they change to a new 'scenario', firmly 'face the music', and just 'play it by ear' – until they 'reach a crashing crescendo', demonstrating that music is 'not their forte'.

'Bandwagons' do, in fact, have a long political history; they come from America, where a mid-nineteenth-century candidate once borrowed the band's vehicle from Barnum's circus so as to enliven his election campaign. The vote-catching value of music was soon recognised, and is still reflected in the proliferation of American campaign songs. The art of 'orchestration' consists of the arrangement and disposition of a score for a variety of instruments; one hopes that composers and arrangers do this *carefully*, but the term 'in a low key' is absurd: in many circumstances a C can sound much higher than a D.* The Wagnerian term 'leitmotif' (really *Leitmotiv*, with a capital L) is best left to specialist writings about Wagner or Wagnerian operas. 'Offbeat' is a vulgar description of the quaintly unusual; what is

---

* The expression 'low key' comes from printed copies of songs, which may be bought in transposed editions for different voices –high, medium and low; and the cover bears this relevant information.

'upbeat' is supposedly desirable and important; and 'downbeat' things are weak and insignificant. In reality it is the *downbeat* that occurs on the first, and usually strongest and most important, part of the bar, and the others are nominally weaker. In conducting, every downbeat must necessarily be preceded by an upbeat.* 'Soft-pedalling' is also a sole-cism: the left pedal on a piano helps to alter the sound but does not necessarily soften it. And the most commonly misused term is the ubiquitous 'crescendo'. Even some music critics get this wrong: "The finale [wrote one], resonant and firm, reached a tremendously stirring crescendo.' The word is Italian and means growing, increasing, advan-cing – in other words getting louder – and the point at which a crescendo is *reached* is more likely to be marked 'piano' or 'pianis-simo'. If it were 'fortissimo' there would be little hope of increased volume. Thus a crescendo may grow and reach a climax, but in itself is only the means to this end.

So much for musical metaphors. But when it comes to the reporting of real musical occasions, or the affairs of musicians, there is one word that immediately springs into newspaper type with a less than mel-odious twang: the ubiquitous 'note', occasionally relieved by a 'chord'. Both are almost invariably 'hit' or 'struck', and can be 'top', 'high', 'low', or 'sour', 'discordant', 'right' or downright 'wrong' notes. 'Hitting the high notes' is always considered to be a sign of great success, even if the story is about a *basso profundo* whose greatest triumphs may spring from the extremely low notes he can hit. Disputes, contracts or mar-riages, however, 'end on a sour note'.

*'Offkey' is meant to convey the impression of bad intonation. Musicians never use the word: they say 'out of tune'; for if something is 'offkey' it has modulated altogether.

Intentional Headline Jokes

Although the *Guardian* is customarily credited with their invention, and certainly has long specialised in them, headline jokes have long been an irresistible temptation for sub-editors as well as printers. The constant wish seems to be to 'get away with it' – in the hope that those in authority will in the heat of production fail to spot an intentional joke or obscenity. When the American newspaper proprietor Randolph Hearst made a speech in which he used the quotation about the superiority of the pen over the sword, one of his compositors purposely misspaced the headline:

Randolph Hearst:

'PEN IS

MIGHTIER

THAN SWORD'

Among the best headline jokes still talked about is the *Guardian*'s report of a bad performance of *Antony and Cleopatra*, headed:

THE BIGGEST ASP DISASTER IN THE WORLD

And in the same paper, an item about a slight mishap in a church organ whose electric blower caught fire, causing the service to be abandoned, was printed under the heading:

HEATED ONE DAY AT THE ORGAN

When the explorer Dr (later Sir) Vivian Fuchs set off on his first Antarctic expedition, the *Liverpool Daily Post* carried the headline:

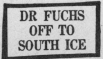

DR FUCHS
OFF TO
SOUTH ICE

... and when, a year later, Fuchs sailed again, the same joke was revived (in both the *Post* and the *Daily Express*):

' Fuchs off again
Sir Vivian Fuchs has sailed from Montevideo on another research and exploration trip to the Antarctic.

City's Starlings Dropping

Vancouver's starling population seems to be dropping, according to a bird count made Saturday.

WOMEN WHO SMOKE HAVE LIGHTER CHILDREN
Doctors' Findings

Dr Spuhler will maintain Swiss role

From KAREL NORSKY
Geneva, January 4
Dr Willy Spuhler, aged 64, today became Switzerland's

Doctors "Rushed Off Feet"
RUN ON MEDICINES

Chinese in car clash

Pyjamaed French Delegates Rush for Chamber

CRUMBLING PILES

Owners held to blame

By our Parliamentary Staff

Disheartening To Doctors
Lack of Openings For Young Men

Henry Moore's marbles

Bees make jam

SWARM of 20,000 bees who had lost their queen settled in the middle of the road and brought traffic to a virtual standstill at the High Street-Vale Road junction, Tunbridge Wells, Kent, today.

His Gas Comes From A Hole
Natural Supply In Area

BALLOON RACE Six Drop Out

NO WATER — SO FIREMEN IMPROVISED

17 Maidens on End

ORGAN TROPHY LOST BY INCHES

GIRL'S STOOL HIGH

From Our Special Correspondent
BLACKPOOL, Tuesday.
A girl, only 5ft. 2in. tall, lost the Edwin Coppock organ solo trophy by three points at the competitive musical festival here to-day. She found too late that the player's stool was adjustable to bring the stops and the pedals within her reach.

IMMIGRATION OFFICERS STOP FLOW OF U.K. SECRETARIES

Farmers in bad odour with townspeople

Acronyms

These are now a regular feature of our daily news, largely because politicans, sociologists, trade unionists, cranks, neophiles, pressure groups, action committees and protest movements of all kinds have become besotted by them. Not only they, but also many fine, praiseworthy (or at any rate unexceptionable) bodies working for the public good, often convey the impression that their founders got together with the principal object of finding a striking acronym, and only then proceeded to choose a name to fit its letters. Acronyms are also the hallmark of aggressively militant bodies in search of notoriety and publicity. For example, when someone sent a few letter-bombs to a medical research establishment, the accompanying anonymous letter said they had come from the 'Animals' Revolutionary Militia (ARM)'. Such terminology suggests the existence of an organisation, with a chairman, officials and a governing committee; and the word 'militia', some kind of irregular army, with commander, officers and soldiers. A free press must report all such occurrences, but in doing so it also gives disproportionate publicity to events that probably sprang from the mind of a single crank with a private grievance.

Acronyms are indeed often memorable (and that, not the saving of time, is their main function) but they are nearly always also ugly, idiotic, and likely to embarrass any sensitive person obliged to utter them. There are some words which *appear* to be acronyms but are not: for example, that excellent organisation, the National Association for Mental Health, unaccountably and perversely calls itself MIND. The *M*ational *I*ssociation for *N*ental *D*ealth? Newspapers regrettably pander to the wishes of trendily acronymic organisations. Even ultra-conservative papers, reporting the activities of revolutionary bodies they despise, dutifully give their full name followed by the acronym in parentheses, whether the full name is repeated in the story or not; and if it is *not* repeated there is clearly no need for the acronym to be stated in the first place. Perhaps they should isolate such idiocies between the implied sarcasm of a pair of quotation-marks.

The word 'acronym' comes from the Greek *acr(o)*, the topmost, the point (or in this case, the beginning), and *onyma*, name. Thus 'acronym' is itself an acronym. The fashioning of easy abbreviations of this kind goes back to the beginning of the twentieth century and started in a mild, harmless and sporadic way. For example, newspaper readers during the First World War would have understood what was meant by the statement 'Anzacs are going awol because they can't take the flak'.*

---

*Australian and New Zealand Army Corps; *absent without leave*; 'Fliegerab-wehrkanonen', i.e. German anti-aircraft guns, or their fire.

But apart from some highly specialised professional acronyms and one or two firms ('Nabisco' was registered by the National Biscuit Company in 1901), they would be found mainly in the armed forces.

It was Russia and Germany (both of them top-heavy bureaucracies long before they turned into officialdom-ridden dictatorships) who started the bureaucratic and political acronym. Not for them simple names like Admiralty, Home Office, Air Ministry or Treasury. Dictatorships must either intimidate the common people with impressively long, official-sounding names, or else mystify them with cabalistic abbreviations. George Orwell's satirical inventions in Nineteen Eighty-Four – 'Thinkpol' (Thought Police), 'Minipax' (Ministry of Peace, i.e. War), 'Ficdep' (the official Department of Fiction), etc. – parodied the language of the Comintern (Communist International). This totalitarian politicisation of language was later eagerly adopted by the 'Nazis' (their own name concocted from Nationalsozialistische Deutsche Arbeiterpartei), who gave the world such unlovely abbreviations as Gestapo (Geheime Staatspolizei) for the secret state police, Schupo (Schutzpolizei) the ordinary police, their Stalags, Oflags – and Kazetts, the gruesome name for concentration camps, being the German pronunciation of the key consonants in Konzentrationslager. The Hitler Youth was known as the Hajott ('Aitch-Jay'), and both the SA and SS were familiar only as abbreviations. Many ordinary Germans may not even have known their true meaning. Thus can a people be led by the nose!

The Russians, of course, still love their acronyms, like Comecon, Gulag and OGPU, and there are many other, less sinister but still characteristic, names throughout the communist world. For example, the Bulgarian state wine export company is called VINIMPEX; and jars of Polish gherkins come from Hortex Polcoop, which is presumably some sort of horticultural Polish exporting co-operative.

Now that words like 'Peoples', 'Union', 'Militia', 'Freedom', 'Front', 'Organisation' and 'Liberation' have become part of every would-be revolutionary's parrot-cry, acronyms ending in PO, FU, UF, etc., have proliferated throughout the world, and words like ZANU, ZUPO, ZAPU, ZIFFRA and ZIPRA (to cite the somewhat limited Zimbabwean and Zambian inventiveness alone) are expected to trip lightly off our tongue in everyday speech. Not mine. To my ears the titles of even the most idealistic band of 'freedom fighters' conjure up visions of squalid dictators; or, at best, sound like the name of the last surviving Marx Brother. The mere fact that the origin of acronyms is so rooted in oppressive politics is surely enough to put any decent person off them altogether. It did not, however, stop the liberating allied forces in Europe, with their FIDO, ASDIC, PLUTO and the short-lived AMGOT, (Allied Military Government of Occupied Territory), coined in 1943. Short-lived, because a Turkish diplomat soon pointed out (when he regained his composure) that it meant something unprintable in his language*. AMGOT was therefore hurriedly replaced by the non-acronymic AMG. The British Women's Royal Naval Service, colloquially, affectionally and near-acronymically known as the Wrens, was at first intended to be called the Women's Auxiliary Naval Corps, 'which would never have done, because they'd have been known as the Wancs', as their original commander engagingly pointed out when she appeared on the BBC programme Woman's Hour. The name of the Wrens' American counterparts, Women Appointed for Volunteer Emergency Services, sounds suspiciously like a creation purposely chosen so as to make the acronym Waves (and it goes without saying that the acronymist feels free to omit any initials that inconveniently stand in his way). But the Commander-in-Chief United States Fleet is still called CINCUS, pronounced 'sink us'. President Nixon's Committee for the Reelection of the President (CREEP) was a bad second-best to the originally intended CRAP: '. . . the American President'.

In Britain acronyms have by tradition played an important part in the trade union movement, at any rate from the first decade or so of the twentieth century. The Amalgamated Railway Servants (always referred to in full, not as ARS) were superseded in 1913 by a rival organisation, the National Union of Railway Servants (NURS); and that, in turn, became the National Union of Railwaymen (NUR) − perhaps a more logical name when the worker became increasingly aware that he is the master, not the servant. Yet the familiar acronym ASLEF still enshrines in it the words 'Footplatemen' and 'Firemen' some hundred years after locomotives stopped having footplates and thirty years after they last had fires to be stoked. The great proliferation of British unions (and their early flirtation with communist Russia) brought in its wake vast numbers of acronyms. One of the latest is SOGAT '82, formed from an existing print union's name to which we are now expected to add an apostrophe and two numerals in solemn public commemoration of the year in which it reorganized itself; and the recent formation of the Electrical, Electronic, Telecommunications and Plumbing Union, EETPU: pronounced 'eat poo'. But of course the pronunciation of acronyms has its own absurd idiosyncrasies which (though not within the brief of this book) are slavishly, and often foolishly, observed by speakers on radio and television. Thus NUPE is not 'newp' but 'new pee'; and COHSE is not pronounced to rhyme with 'foes' but like 'cosy' (which it patently is not). And hardly a day passes when the Arbitration and Conciliation Advisory Service (ACAS) is not in the news: the name presumably chosen with the pronunciation 'ache-ass' in mind.

---

*Every Turkish waiter I questioned about the meaning of AMGOT laughed − but refused to translate. So did the cultural attaché of the Embassy; and, when he had stopped laughing, said, 'No such word in Turkish.' But there is no place for coyness in a dictionary, and I am grateful to the BBC Turkish Service for giving me the precise English vernacular equivalent: am='cunt'+göt='arse'.

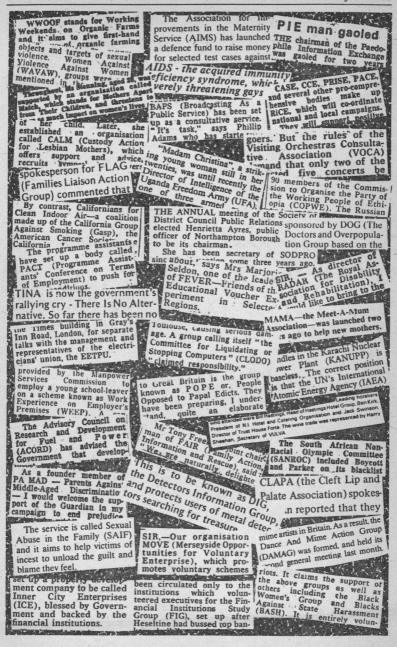

WWOOF stands for Working Weekends on Organic Farms and it aims to give first-hand objects and targets of sexual violence. Women Against Women (WAVAW), groups were mentioned in ... biennial, aged 28, was supported by an organisation called Match, which stands for Mothers Apart from their Children, and threatens to ... much impact on women's lives of her child. Later, she established an organisation called CALM (Custody Action for Lesbian Mothers), which offers support and advice, recruits ... spokesperson for FLAG (Families Liaison Action Group) commented that

By contrast, Californians for Clean Indoor Air—a coalition made up of the California Group Against Smoking (Gasp), the American Cancer Society, California ...
The programme assistants e have set up a body called PACT (Programme Assistants' Conference on Terms of Employment) to push for ...

TINA is now the government's rallying cry - There Is No Alternative. So far there has been no ...

...the Times building in Gray's Inn Road, London, for separate talks with the management and representatives of the electricians' union, the EETPU.

...provided by the Manpower Services Commission to employ a young school-leaver on a scheme known as Work Experience on Employer's Premises (WEEP). A ...

The Advisory Council on Research and Development for Fuel and Power (ACORD) has advised the Government that develop ...

As a founder member of PA MAD — Parents Against Middle-Aged Discrimination — I would welcome the support of the Guardian in my campaign to end prejudice ...

The service is called Sexual Abuse in the Family (SAIF) and it aims to help victims of incest to unload the guilt and blame they feel.

...set up a property development company to be called Inner City Enterprises (ICE), blessed by Government and backed by the financial institutions.

The Association for Improvements in the Maternity Service (AIMS) has launched a defence fund to raise money for selected test cases against

AIDS - the acquired immunity deficiency syndrome, which verely threatening gays

BAPS (Broadcasting As a Public Service) has been set up as a consultative service. "It's task," says Phillip Adams who has started ...

"Madam Christina" a strik ing young woman still in her twenties, was until recently the Director of Intelligence of the Uganda Freedom Army (UFA), one of three armed ...

THE ANNUAL meeting of the Society of ... District Council Public Relations elected Henrietta Ayres, public officer of Northampton Borough to be its chairman.
She has been secretary of SODPRO ... some three years ago. sinc about," says Mrs Marjori Seldon, one of the leade of FEVER—Friends of the Educational Voucher Ex periment in Selecte Regions.

Toulouse, causing serious damage. A group calling itself "the Committee for Liquidating or Stopping Computers" (CLODO) "claimed responsibility."

...to Great Britain is the group known as POPE or, People Opposed to Papal Edicts. They have been preparing, I under stand, quite an elaborate

Mr Tony Free man of FAIR (Family Action, Information and Rescue), joint chair "We are naturally" delighte

This is to be known as DIG, the Detectors Information Group, and protects users of metal detectors searching for treasure

SIR,—Our organisation MOVE (Merseyside Opportunities for Voluntary Enterprise), which promotes voluntary schemes

...been circulated only to the institutions which volunteered executives for the Financial Institutions Study Group (FIG), set up after Heseltine had bussed top ban-

PIE man gaoled
THE chairman of the Paedo phile Information Exchange was gaoled for two years

CASE, CCE, PRISE, PACE, and several other pro-compre hensive bodies make up RiCE, which will co-ordinate national and local campaigns. They will support positive ... goers. But the rules of the Visiting Orchestras Consultative Association (VOCA) ...mand that only two of the ...ted five concerts be 90 members of the Commission to Organise the Party of the Working People of Ethiopia (COPWE). The Russian ... sponsored by DOG (The Doctors and Overpopulation Group based on the ...

SIR, — As director of RADAR (The Royal Association for Disability and Rehabilitation), I ...uld like to bring to the

MAMA—the Meet-A-Mum Association—was launched two is ago to help new mothers.

...ndles in the Karachi Nuclear ...wer Plant (KANUPP) is baseless. The correct position is that the UN's International Atomic Energy Agency (IAEA) ...

who attended were Bill Hastings, Head of Hastings Hotel Group, Ben Kirk, President of N.I. Hotel and Catering Organisation and Jack Swinson, Director of Trust House Forte. The wine trade was represented by Harry Sheehan, Secretary of VULVA

The South African Non-Racial Olympic Committee (SANROC) included Boycott and Parker on its blacklist

CLAPA (the Cleft Lip and Palate Association) spokes ...n reported that they

mime artists in Britain. As a result, the Dance And Mime Action Group (DAMAG) was formed, and held its ...ond general meeting last month.

riots. It claims the support of the above groups as well as others including the Black Women's Group and Blacks Against State Harassment (BASH). It is entirely volun-

The Gasping Adverbial Opener

Basically, there is nothing wrong with initial adverbs except repeated over-use — especially the opening word of this paragraph, a word which is at present enjoying an epidemic popularity; and even that opening would be better rephrased 'There is nothing basically wrong with initial adverbs', or the adverb omitted altogether. What is tedious, however, is the adverbial opener used as a kind of springboard for ideas. Like the ubiquitous spoken 'Basically ...' (followed by a thought-collecting pause), which is little more than a throat-clearing noise, the written adverbial opener followed by a great gasping comma is like a motor-car whose engine stalls as soon as it is put into gear. One imagines a journalist winding a piece of blank paper into his typewriter, tapping out an adverb, adding a comma, and waiting for inspiration. If the Book of Genesis were to be rewritten in Fleet Street it would begin:

> INITIALLY, God created the heaven and the earth. BASICALLY, the earth was without form, and void: NOTICEABLY, darkness was upon the face of the deep. REPORTEDLY, the spirit of God moved upon the waters. LOFTILY, God said, Let there be light. PREDICTABLY, there was light. BRILLIANTLY, God called the light Day and, ADDITIONALLY, the darkness he called Night. CURIOUSLY, God created man in His own image ... STARTLINGLY, male and female created He them ... THANKFULLY, God saw everything that He had made: and, INTERESTINGLY, it was good. SUBSEQUENTLY, the evening and the morning were the sixth day ... etc.

Fleet Street has flogged the adverbial opener to death. It was also a favourite of Bible translators in the sixteenth century: I lost count at about a hundred admonitions in the New Testament beginning with 'VERILY, I say unto ye'. However anyone aspiring to an easily readable style will try to remove the dangling adverb from the beginning and tuck it, if he really needs it, somewhere inside the sentence. His prose will also be less prone to confusion: 'Ironically, he was writing government propaganda' or 'Sadly, she died before her son became famous' leaves us ignorant of who or what was ironical or sad.

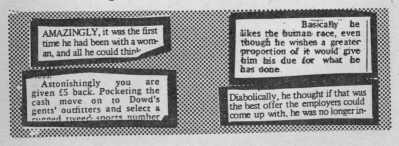

AMAZINGLY, it was the first time he had been with a woman, and all he could thin~

Astonishingly you are given £5 back. Pocketing the cash move on to Dowd's gents' outfitters and select a rugged tweed sports number

Basically he likes the human race, even though he wishes a greater proportion of it would give him his due for what he has done.

Diabolically, he thought if that was the best offer the employers could come up with, he was no longer in-

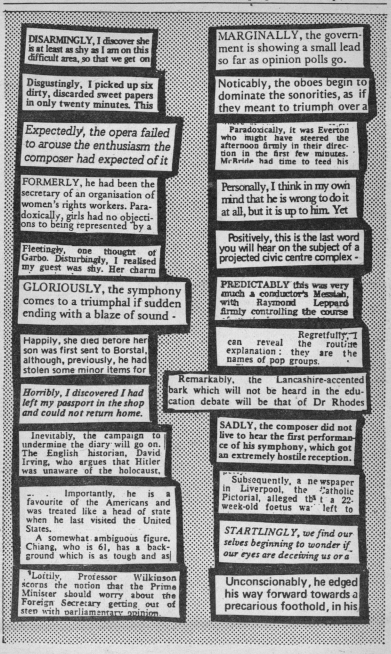

DISARMINGLY, I discover she is at least as shy as I am on this difficult area, so that we get on

Disgustingly, I picked up six dirty, discarded sweet papers in only twenty minutes. This

Expectedly, the opera failed to arouse the enthusiasm the composer had expected of it

FORMERLY, he had been the secretary of an organisation of women's rights workers. Paradoxically, girls had no objections to being represented by a

Fleetingly, one thought of Garbo. Disturbingly, I realised my guest was shy. Her charm

GLORIOUSLY, the symphony comes to a triumphal if sudden ending with a blaze of sound -

Happily, she died before her son was first sent to Borstal, although, previously, he had stolen some minor items for

Horribly, I discovered I had left my passport in the shop and could not return home.

Inevitably, the campaign to undermine the diary will go on. The English historian, David Irving, who argues that Hitler was unaware of the holocaust,

_. . Importantly, he is a favourite of the Americans and was treated like a head of state when he last visited the United States.
A somewhat ambiguous figure. Chiang, who is 61, has a background which is as tough and as

Loftily, Professor Wilkinson scorns the notion that the Prime Minister should worry about the Foreign Secretary getting out of step with parliamentary opinion.

MARGINALLY, the government is showing a small lead so far as opinion polls go.

Noticably, the oboes begin to dominate the sonorities, as if they meant to triumph over a

Paradoxically, it was Everton who might have steered the afternoon firmly in their direction in the first few minutes. McBride had time to feed his

Personally, I think in my own mind that he is wrong to do it at all, but it is up to him. Yet

Positively, this is the last word you will hear on the subject of a projected civic centre complex -

PREDICTABLY this was very much a conductor's Messiah, with Raymond Leppard firmly controlling the course

Regretfully, I can reveal the routine explanation : they are the names of pop groups.

Remarkably, the Lancashire-accented bark which will not be heard in the education debate will be that of Dr Rhodes

SADLY, the composer did not live to hear the first performance of his symphony, which got an extremely hostile reception.

Subsequently, a newspaper in Liverpool, the Catholic Pictorial, alleged that a 22-week-old foetus was left to

STARTLINGLY, we find ourselves beginning to wonder if our eyes are deceiving us or a

Unconscionably, he edged his way forward towards a precarious foothold, in his

Hyphens Are Optional

'The primary function of the hyphen is to indicate that two or more words are to be read together as a single word with its own meaning.'

FOWLER'S MODERN ENGLISH USAGE

Thanks to falling standards in schools, trendy teachers and would-be educational reformers, spelling is becoming freer and more haphazard each year, as more and more products of their 'liberal' education spill on to the market. So it is hardly surprising that punctuation, too, suffers. Commas are pressed into service in place of full-stops. The useful semicolon and colon are almost forgotten: you may search through page after page of even the most august literary weekly without encountering either. Hyphens are either misunderstood or treated as optional extras — to the detriment of sense and meaning. Newspaper readers are generally in a hurry. If a sentence has to be read several times before the writer's meaning becomes clear, then the writer has failed to communicate efficiently with his public.

'After finishing school in Paris' or 'After finishing-school'? A 'cross section' or 'cross-section' of the population? Blue-tits or blue tits? A hot dog salesman? Or was he selling hot-dogs? Were there no-waiting signs or no waiting signs? Is the pro vice chancellor in favour of vice? Are sheep worrying about sheep-worrying? Does she teach seventy odd children, or seventy-odd? Is the Duke of Edinburgh fond of wild-life, or wild life? Why is the Obscene Publications Squad not prosecuted for being obscene? What is superfluous about the superfluous hair remover? What made the sick bed sick? Is he the best Russian speaker or the best Russian-speaker?

In the words of the tabloid leader-writer, 'We demand to know!'

The marshes at Havengate Island are gradually getting saltier and this is threatening the existence of the water-flies, beatles, and other insects which live in the mud and on which the avocets feed.

studying music. When he went up to Oxford, he read English philogy, and perhaps one reason why his parents seem to have been so unpercentive lies in the fact that

Town Hall), Mr Foot delivered on Saturday the same speech for the 41st time.

This stupendous fete of stamina was greeted, as throughout the North and Midlands, with rapturous adoration. "Forty-first Fabulous Night of footage!" This guaranteed show stopper is hauling in huge crowds.

CONTRAVERSIAL artist Bryan Organ has been commissioned to paint the first official portrait of Lady Diana Spencer.

But the last word went to Diana Dors. Someone wanted to know if their would be a nubile girl to do the exercises and titillate the male viewers.

Sheep worrying: appeal to dog owners

A hot dog salesman was led away with an eye gashed and bleeding after about 50 youths overturned his stall.

DO YOU WANT A WOMAN VICAR?

INTERESTING TALL BOYS AT JAMES ADAM'S SALE

The King had five foot soldiers and six cross bow men with him wherever he travelled.

ZAIRE'S flamboyant, currently troubled President Mobuto, took Mr Huang Hua, Chinese Foreign Minister for a ride in his leopard skin-seated helicopter yesterday to ...ier arrival was greeted by a fly past of the islands' three Dakotas and the hoots and sirens of a small armada of yachts who went out to meet Britannia and her escort ship HMS Antrim.

HORSE BACK UP SNOWDON

Giant pay out bid to beat court

DOCTORS REVIEW BODY

ANTI-PAY BED BOARD IS TO B ABOLISHED

● Approved School-master IVOR COOK: "I was snubbed by my colleagues."

..."vigilantes" would take the law into their own hands over the murder of a homosexual Turkish bath attendant.

When he returned, he said there had been clear evidence of sheep rustling on the mountainside.

AWARD FOR ANTI-SNAKE BITE RESEARCH

The Carl Davis-William Rushton musical thriller, "Sir Harry North's Last Case", won its laughs, though heaven help anyone who has to hear this ...ergraduate-type pastiche a...

Whilst appreciating that large new organisations will have settling in problems, this flooring defect is an obvious danger of...

New help on sick notes

From his sick bed, Wigan Infirmary Andy, his body a mass of bumps and bruises, said: "I don't remember the accident, it happened so quickly...

Charles Rupert Moore, stained glass designer and aeronautical artist, died on ...uly 21. He was 77.

...at ...and among the assembled guests were the mayor and many other big wigs who seemed to enjoy a...

Delight on the faces of Dirk Treber, chairman of the Hesse environmental party, and his running mate, Priska Hinz, after the election results were announced.

THE 500 francs costs imposed on Olympic ath-...ete Sebastian Coe after a Lakeside punch up in Swit-...zerland will be paid by the organisers of the Zurich athletics meeting.

UNIVERSITY OF MANCHESTER
DEPARTMENT OF EXTRA MURAL STUDIES

Words-plitting

If we are no longer taught Greek or Latin, and how words are made, we cannot be expected to divide them into their component parts when it becomes necessary to split a word at the end of a line. The advent of computer typesetting has only made things worse, although some systems in the new technology are now able to have correct spelling and word-splitting facilities programmed into them. Each one of the examples illustrated here would be described as a 'bad break'.

He attacked five cars and a bungalow, smashing winds-creens and windows and doing damage totalling £456.

Because of the country's difficult economic condi-tion, at a time when rear-mament was taking place, he told Ministers they should take a cut in salary,

live in, for example, the con-stituency of Newham South, you should address your let-ter to "The Member for Ne-wham South, Members' Lob-by, The County Hall, Lon-don SE1 7PB."

schemes in Northern Ire-land wouldn't it be better to do so without subsidis-ing the extravagant lifes-tyle of a lot of American con men?"

THE DOOR was yesterday slammed shut on Shirley Williams — and her hopes of a Parliamentary com-eback.

them what they meant. "We think it more likely than not some of the existing wor-kforce could not read the signs when they started;

dently still continues, of recruit-ing its nudes from the English lower-middle classes, long-lim-bed girls from Lytham St Anne's

wich. He has pleaded not guilty to six charges of. def-rauding the National Health Service by exaggerating the role the consultant played in the practice.

..... when he was arrested, was yester-day jailed for six months at Sheffield for sho-plifting.

A plumber has died after jumping naked from the third floor bedroom of his girlf-riend's apartment to escape from the enraged husband who

The jury took just over four hours to clear Calder of murder, but they found his guilty of involuntary mans-laughter and he was given a

of enthusiasm, to interrupt her defiant stare with a flicker of collusive smile? This American artist was a bew-itching Rosina, teasing, capri-cious, delightful to look at and listen to, with her agile colora-

Sovereignty for false gods. widsom for hear-taches.

General de Gaulle was our wise man and told us "non." Let it be that on June 5.

makers are among the victims, with 30 to 40 handbags snatched each day in the bus-tling resort of Torremolinos.

A police sergeant who did not report to his superiors a sexual assault on a girl aged eight, because of his position as a bishop in the Mormon Church, said yesterday that he had been made

He was a collector for Zetters Coupons, Ltd, and took money ·from syndicate subscribers, made the match selections, and entered the coupon for them.

Weekend's *Skin* team. The content will be aimed primarily at Asians one week, Afro-Caribbeans the next.

The book is suitable for children as well as grownups, although the first

centre-half Keith Eddy had to drop out with a hamstring strain suffered in train-

This is considered one of the loopholes, together with many others.

Charles had bought Allibar to press ahead with his horseracing career. "The Queen has

The moratorium is to be replaced by "a period of stringent discipline" and is itself a small victory for Mr

Back, content, we went from our picnic to the hushed press-box for the afternoon's play. I murmured to grey sandwich nibbler

co-operative discount warehouses on Stockholm's outskirts. They vanished with about 4·1 million crowns (£424.000)

The Russians went into Afghanistan because they could not tolerate an unstable state on their border and sought to resolve its political problems by establishing a compliant government walking to Moscow's heel.

Died. Edgar Snow, 66, preeminent American journalist specializing in Chinese affairs (*see* THE PRESS).

"I am completely deflated," he said yesterday. The organisers' attitude was "petty-minded."

thought he had already killed his sister Jill and her boyfriend Roland. a Cumbrian farmer. after telling her that

Plump and jolly in an open-neck striped shirt and with his hands in perpetual mtion. Mr

The moratorium is to be replaced by "a period of stringent discipline" and is itself a small victory for Mr

retreat in the cosiness of one's home, or in the chandelier-lit elegance of St John's, Smith Square. And what cosier way to begin than with Vaughan Williams's *Songs of*

times on Wednesday. He had connected a 220-volt electric cord to the screwdriver to torture them, police said.

IN A WEEK which promises to belong to the Social Democrats, the Government was last night facing yet another

year. He had a job with the Munich-based Radio Free Europe and it was his outspoken commentaries about events n Bulgaria. broadcast on

past. He had 14 convictions for offences including handling gelignite. aggravated burglary. possessing firearms, and conspiracy to rob.

Oh, What a Cover-up of the Bare Facts

There are certain conventions concerning nakedness which the press rigorously observes. The word 'naked' itself is taboo: 'nude' is the only proper newspaper description of anyone not wearing clothes. Adam and Eve were naked, but 'page three girlies' are nude. Nakedness is for children, unclothed adults are nude, and lewd. Nudists are given the stilted euphemism 'naturists'. They are welcomed on a few English beaches – elsewhere they get 'the cold shoulder'. A 'big cover-up' may be ordered; or they get a 'dressing-down' and are 'stripped' of the opportunity to 'bare all'.

In the early 1970s an exhibitionist trick became fashionable, when young persons took to running naked through streets or other public places for no other reason than to scandalise onlookers and gain press publicity. Longman's Dictionary of Contemporary English (1970) was the first to define 'streaking', and adds to its definition the pedantically correct information, '. . . with no clothes on, except possibly the feet or head.' One essential thing about streaking is that it happens very quickly (like 'streaked lightning'? Or perhaps it is related to an old breed of dog known as the streaker); another, that it is asexual in intent, unlike the form of exhibitionism known as 'flashing', which (I am reliably informed) does not necessarily happen with great speed. This is also a new word, not given even in the 1972 Oxford English Dictionary supplement except in its other, established meanings; these, including the cricketing one ('a fielder who chases balls outside the off-stump') and the motor-car direction indicators (now 'winkers'), are now being avoided for fear of misunderstandings. When a 'flasher' is arrested and brought to court, he is described as having 'exposed his person'. I believe this is not a press euphemism but an old legal one for the penis – and one which every defence lawyer should be able to demolish by pointing out that the judge is also exposing his 'person', in court. The police officer arresting a streaker invariably tries to cover his or her nakedness with some garment or object (in one case his helmet), 'strategically placed'. In fact, STRATEGIC PLACES← in the tabloid papers are almost always sexual.

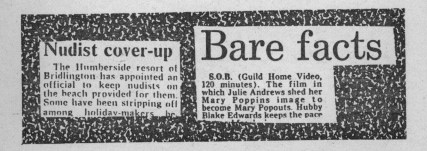

Nudist cover-up

The Humberside resort of Bridlington has appointed an official to keep nudists on the beach provided for them. Some have been stripping off among holiday-makers. bc

Bare facts

S.O.B. (Guild Home Video, 120 minutes). The film in which Julie Andrews shed her Mary Poppins image to become Mary Popouts. Hubby Blake Edwards keeps the pace

Bare facts

ANTHONY CLARE

ANATOMY OF NAKEDNESS by Paul Ableman. Orbis, 112pp, £7·95.

Bare facts

PAGE THREE girls start young, the nearer to 16 the better, but can they last the distance, asks Guardian Women. Page 10.

The bare truth of holiday hotel

Nudists think they're covered

THERE are changes afoot at a Liverpool Naturist club. For the Liverpool Sun and Air Society has applied for permission to extend its grounds and build up to 30 huts and caravans... as extra changing accommodation. The Knowsley nature-lovers face a dressing down from

Bare facts

Advertisements for £200 - a - week nude roles in the West End attracted just five hopefuls. Stanley Reynolds explores the full-frontal backlash.

Nude gets the cold shoulder

ANTICS on the beach were all together

WHAT A COVER UP

Naturists are giving Brighton's official nudist beach a cold shoulder tomorrow, the opening day. " You cannot trust the weather at this time of year ", Mr Ernest Stanley, chairman of the Kent and Sussex Association of Sun Clubs, said.

Nudist stripped of office wins through

By IAN GLOVER-JAMES

A GARAGE owner's wife who was stripped of her office in the Girls' Brigade because she was a nudist has set up her own breakaway group.

NOBODY could have any doubt yesterday that Alan Margolis loves Penny Wise. He flashed it from the roof tops.

BARE TRUTH CURBED BY PAY ROW

Sex offenders are being stopped from facing the bare truth at a top Hampshire hospital—all because of the health workers pay row.

Men who continually expose themselves in front of women have been going to Park Prewett Psychiatric Hospital in Basingstoke—and walking nde in a room in front of six married women medical staff including nurses from COHSE. But now it has been stopped because it is not regarded as " emergency treatment."

COMRADES COVER UP

EVERY year Moscow gets a few scorching days. Then the boys and girls flock to the swimming pools and recreation areas. And of course, it being a

Bare truth about fashion exploits

MODELS in see-through blouses are being used by top fashion firms who are

The Black-on-White Misprint Show

A generation ago a misprint in a newspaper was rare, and a misspelling even rarer. If such a typographical accident produced some humorous word or drastically changed meaning, men would lovingly preserve the cutting and carefully take it, tattered and crumbling, from their wallet to delight their friends. An amusing or suggestive misprint was piquant enough; but when there was evidence of ribald sabotage, delight knew no bounds. When, for example, Queen Victoria opened the new Waterloo Bridge in London, The Times is said to have reported that she was 'the first personage to piss over the bridge'.

There was a notorious interpolation of an obscenity in the same newspaper's edition of 23 January 1882, page seven, column four. The entire page, printed in a typeface so small and lines so closely spaced that it is barely possible to read it without a magnifying-glass, was devoted to a report of preceedings in the House of Commons. It is unrelieved by ornament or illustration, and contains over 10,000 words devoted to a speech (mostly verbatim but with occasional passages in précis) by the Home Secretary, Sir William Harcourt. The burning question at the time concerned tenant farmers in Yorkshire, and the speech was impassioned, rhetorical and long. Almost exactly halfway through the parliamentary report, a wicked compositor interpolated the words, 'The speaker then said he felt inclined for a bit of fucking. I think that is very likely. (Laughter.)' Probably sarcasm as well as ribaldry was intended. For, near the end of his marathon oration, Sir William had said: 'Well, gentlemen, I have detained you too long. (Cries of "No", "Go on", and "Loud Cheers")', which perhaps strained the patience of the typesetter to breaking-point. For three days the newspaper kept silent, hoping that no one had noticed. But on 27 January the following paragraph appeared, set in far larger type than the fateful speech, bigger even than the news, below it, of a 'shocking mine accident' and a 'daring jewel robbery':

No pains have been spared by the management of this journal to discover the author of a gross outrage committed by the interpolation of a line in the speech of Sir William Harcourt reported in our issue of Monday last. This malicious fabrication was surreptitiously introduced shortly before the paper went to press. The matter is now under legal investigation, and it is hoped that the perpetrator of the outrage will be brought to punishment.

THE TIMES, MONDAY, JANUARY 23, 1882.

7

The fateful page 7 of *The Times*, 23 January 1882.

The perpetrator of the outrage was never brought to justice. And on 12 June he struck again, in an advertisement for a book entitled *Everyday Life in Our Public Schools*, to which the rogue compositor added the spurious subtitle 'A Disquisition upon Fucking'. This time *The Times* chose to keep a dignified silence, and the miscreant called it a day. But for years afterwards it was the rule that a newspaper compositor whose employment was terminated, whether by the paper or himself, did not work out his notice but received the appropriate pay-off and left immediately. Editors were unwilling to face the risk of devil-may-care sabotage.

Accidental misprints were almost unknown. Before the advent of mechanical typesetting, every single letter was assembled by hand into a 'typestick' and thence transferred to a 'forme': a laborious, time-consuming and eye-straining task; yet the very slowness of the work meant that slapdash typesetting was practically eliminated. Besides, compositors were members of a proud and ancient craft-guild who took pride in their work and had conscientiousness drummed into them during long years of apprenticeship.

Then, in 1888, was patented Linotype, a mechanical method of typesetting by keyboard, comprising a machine process of casting letters and spaces into a solid line of type. All the compositor had in front of him was the copy and his keyboard. If his fingers hit a wrong key he usually did not know about it, as the process of casting was carried on inside the machine (though he could, of course, stop to look at a cast 'slug' as it emerged). Thus there would have been every excuse for a greater number of misprints. But the combined skills of compositor and proof-reader saw to it that errors were rare.

The 'new technology' works in a different manner. The Linotype keyboard has been abandoned, and typesetting machines are fitted with the ordinary QWERTYUIOP arrangements of keys which can be as quickly mastered as an ordinary typewriter. There is also a VDU, or visual display unit – a television screen on which the words appear as they are typed. Correction is simple and immediate, as the work does not have to be printed out until all mistakes have been eliminated. Amendments and corrections can also be made on the galley proof. One would therefore expect that thanks to this new technology misprints would be rarer than ever. Unfortunately the opposite is true. There is not a single issue, probably not a single page, of a daily newspaper which is not liberally strewn with errors of spelling or grammar. The reason lies partly in the lamentable decline of educational standards (with their emphasis on trendy 'free expression' in place of grammar, and the dismissal of Latin and Greek as 'dead' languages); and partly in the system of recruitment dictated by the print unions. For although an editor or newspaper manager can interview applicants for a com-positor's job, and choose the one he considers most proficient, it is the shop steward who has the ultimate power of hiring whomever he may choose. And as comps are still among the biggest wage-earners in Fleet

(Ballynaicign) replied favourably to the first question, and on the second said he would use his influence to ensure the preservation of the Lord's Dad.

In their report to the British Dental Association the doctors say that teeth and bums of the apple - eaters were in considerably better condition during the test than those of the "control" group.

M R KERRY PACKER claimed in the High Court in London yesterday that the governing bodies of English and international cricket ar being "used to fight Australia's battle" over the "super Testes."

In addition, the skilled public speaker will avoid the habit of trying to underline his points by means of excessive testiculation. An almost infallible way to

Mr Wilkinson said he was then confronted by three men with stocking masks and iron bras.

Dead-eye Stewart Fraser, who got three against the league of Ireland recently, attempted a shit from 20 yards, but was so wide of the target that he actually found Carlyle with his attempt. The outside-right was so surprised at the "pass" that he made a mess of his shot at goal.

Lord Bowels
dies at 68

Lord Bowles, formerly Mr Francis George Bowles, who resigned as M.P. for the Nuneaton.

Miranda—now Lady Nuttal: —said in Miami: "I was awoken at 5.30 in the morning by a soft football on the carpet.
"I sat up to find this man in the room moving about."

A five month drought in the Eastern grain planting provinces has meant that the Soviets are unlikely to have a good crap this year.

LONDON — Britons are becoming experts on their neighbours love making habits — because of the flimsy partitions between modern houses.
Anthony Cadman, Director-General of the Brick Development Association, believes that people will only be able to keep their sex lives private if walls made of timber and plasterbord are replaced with solid — and more expensive — prick partitions.

The proceedings ended with a rousing rendering of the Eton Beating Song. After the ceremo

LONELY / UNATTACHED. Meet the incest people locally and discreetly through the highly recommended service of Kate's intro Bureau.

Mi : Faithfull, 22-years-old girl-fiend of Rolling Stone Mick Jagger, spoke briefly to her mother who met her for about 30 minutes.

A couple seeking a divorce would, after filing a petition, have to appear before a judge in chambers who would consider arrangements made for the children. The shit would only proceed to a decree nisi if the judge was satisfied that the best possible arrangements had been made.

Street, nepotism is rife. Near-dyslexia rules KO. There are compositors in Fleet Street who set type for a few lucrative hours each week but who are really taxi-drivers or unskilled labourers by trade; and their spelling and general literacy may be more like that one might expect from an unschooled taxi-driver than a supposedly skilled print-worker. Many of them work only a few hours at night and (like many other semi-skilled Fleet Street workers) are classed as part-time, casual labourers. Until recently they simply signed for their cash payments with false names like Mickey Mouse or D. Duck – and for years got away without paying income tax.

But you will not read of this sorry state of affairs in your favourite newspaper. Any attempt on the part of editors or journalists to write about it has always been met with a refusal to 'handle', i.e. typeset, such inconvenient truths. This is, of course, a tribute to the stranglehold the print unions have on Fleet Street. The industry is in a precarious financial state, and editors often find it expedient to submit to union censorship rather than lose several million copies.

Let us for a moment liken typesetting, spelling and grammar to musical performance. Before the last war, the Royal Liverpool Philhar-monic Orchestra, for example, consisted of mostly part-time, non-symphonic musicians who played in a dozen or so concerts each season. Between these engagements they made a precarious living by teaching, playing in seaside, music-hall or ships' bands, by selling insurance – or driving taxis. Their playing was competent, although perhaps no better than their semi-professional status would lead one to expect. Today, every symphonic musician is a specialist in his field. Musical standards have risen to such a degree that a wrong note or false entry (known as a 'domino' in the profession) is about as rare and remarkable as a misprint was in *The Times* in 1882. A player who persistently gets things wrong is taken to one side by the leader, conductor or manager (at first informally but later in the presence of the Musicians' Union shop steward) and warned to improve his work, or else his contract could be terminated. This is accepted by players and union alike, for musicians take pride in carrying out their job to the best of their ability. The public does not pay to hear handfuls of wrong notes, or to be obliged to guess a composer's intentions because of a middle-man's incompetence. Nor should newspaper readers have to put up with the shabby, shoddy and slapdash standards now obtaining in Fleet Street. If there were as many wrong notes in a concert by the London Philharmonic Orchestra as there are misprints in every copy of *The Times*, *Telegraph* or *Guardian*, professional musicians would be laughed off the stage.

The only saving grace in this sorry state of affairs is that such crass incompetence (in what is after all the perpetrators' mother-tongue and should come as naturally as sleeping or breathing) occasionally pro-duces results of unintentionally inspired lunacy.

Things that might have been . . . .

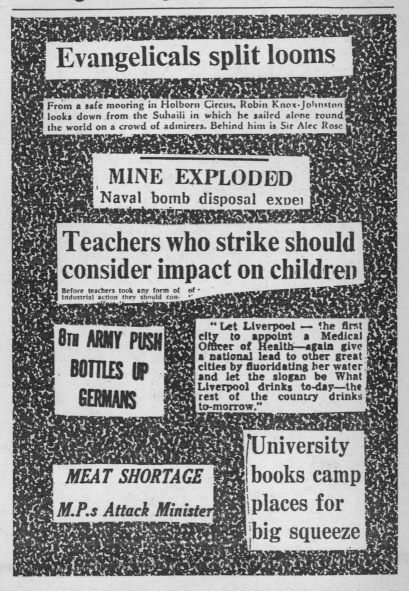

Evangelicals split looms

From a safe mooring in Holborn Circus, Robin Knox-Johnston looks down from the Suhaili in which he sailed alone round the world on a crowd of admirers. Behind him is Sir Alec Rose

MINE EXPLODED
Naval bomb disposal exper

Teachers who strike should consider impact on children

Before teachers took any form of of
industrial action they should con- ''

8TH ARMY PUSH BOTTLES UP GERMANS

"Let Liverpool — the first city to appoint a Medical Officer of Health—again give a national lead to other great cities by fluoridating her water and let the slogan be What Liverpool drinks to-day—the rest of the country drinks to-morrow."

MEAT SHORTAGE

M.P.s Attack Minister

University books camp places for big squeeze

THE toilets at the Harry Pollitt Memorial Youth Centre are nearly complete. Book now for socials, schools, work weekends, etc. Details: 16 King St., WC2-or 01-504 9367.

BRITAIN'S universities don't have a single woman in a chief administrative post, like vice-chancellor. Ten per cent of the academic staff are

MAN FOUND IN MERSEY

Wallasey Police issued the following description of a man whose body was recovered from the Mersey, near New Brighton, yesterday morning: Age between 30 and 40, 5ft. 9in. tall, good build, tattoo on left forearm of woman kneeling on a chair holding a fan, wearing dark striped suit, two print shirts, woollen vest, grey socks and black boots. The

CHURCH CHOIRS

Sir—Your correspondent is wrong in blaming organists for the dearth of choirboys. The fact is that the boys are not to be had. Even to employ bribery and corruption will not attract them.

AN 18-year-old girl accused of stealing a jar of vanishing cream has since disappeared, Huddersfield magistrates were told yesterday.

Parveen Akter, has not been traced, and the summons has not been

IT WAS HANGING OVER HIS HEAD

"It has been hanging over by head. It is quite a relief to get rid of it," said Mr. William Walton, when he was given a conditional discharge at Ipswich Magistrates' Court today.

Walton, of Kemball Street, who is 77, pleaded not guilty to a charge of indecent exposure.

Queen sees Fonteyn take 10 curtains

A NEW £250,000 sewage treatment works for Chipping Norton got under way on Monday when County Councillor Oliver Colston performed a brief inaugural ceremony.

Sergeant Gibson was hit on the head, Constable Hope on the arm. Constable Campbell, in the back seat, escaped injury.

LADY MARY BYNG ENGAGED

GUARDS FIANCE

.... better expressed.

Swooping Coppers, Pouncing Pigs and the Law

'Your British policemen are wonderful' is a common saying attributed to tourists; but wonderful as they are, they have laboured under the nickname of 'pigs' for longer than they have been called policemen. The OED dates the earliest use of 'pigs' 1810, when they were still Bow Street Runners (after the famous police station and magistrates' court in London), and before Sir Robert Peel, twice Home Secretary between 1822 and 1830, formed the nucleus of the modern police force in 1829. They derived their two most common and affectionate nicknames, 'peelers' and 'bobbies', from Peel's name. But they had already become 'peelers' in Ireland by 1817, when Peel, as Secretary of State for Ireland, was in charge of law and order there. 'Bobby' has survived, whereas 'peeler' died with the nineteenth century. 'Pig' was sometimes varied to 'grunter' among thieves, but then, thieves have always been good at inventing nicknames and slang that would help to keep secrets from the ears of law-abiding folk.

It is tempting but inaccurate to link 'grunter' and 'pig' with the modern 'copper', although all three are old nicknames for coins as well as policemen: 'grunter' was a shilling (5p), 'pig' a sixpenny piece (abolished in 1980, when it was worth 2½p). A police 'copper' is one who 'cops' someone, i.e. arrests him; and that meaning, as well as the saying 'It's a fair cop', has existed since the early eighteenth century, long before policemen. Politer usage gives every policeman the honorary rank of 'officer', which is correct insofar as even the most junior cadet is a holder of certain authority and office. But it is generally used only to flatter him. To call him 'constable' is tantamount to the patronising address 'my good man'. The British policemen's uniform is black (at any rate to the naked eye), but they are colloquially known as 'the Boys in Blue'.

Police ('some of them armed' is nowadays a frequent and invariable phrase following the word) tend to refer to people by their own special words, like 'elements' (usually 'undesirable', 'rowdy', 'riotous' or otherwise unpleasant) or 'characters'; and their investigations (or 'probes') may turn into 'cases' (short for 'law cases'). When they, or lawyers, decide to start proceedings, they are said by the press to 'act': a usefully short word for headlines. Recurring news phrases include 'police are satisfied that it is a case of murder' (an odd way of reporting deeds that should cause no satisfaction at all) and 'a man is helping police with enquiries' (a way of avoiding the presumption of guilt and in no way implying helpfulness on the suspect's part).

Other euphemisms include the old favourite of the News of the World (which was once alone in the frank reporting of sex cases), 'She was not interfered with', often with absurdly paradoxical effect.

Americans have an offence called 'statutory rape', which is occasionally thus reported in British papers without the explanation that it is an abbreviated American legal term, not a form of rape obligatory by statute. And there is the offence of 'unlawful sexual intercourse', meaning with a person under the age of consent. 'Forcible rape' is surely a tautology.

Most such cliché euphemisms are designed to pay regard to the old English legal truism that a man is innocent until proved guilty. Here the word 'allege' is almost indispensable. It comes from the Latin *ad* + *legare*, the action of making a charge before a court (until the seventeenth century a man who did such a thing was officially known as an *allegator*, but the advent of zoos presumably put an end to that), and its use implies that no proof has been established either way.

Illicit drugs are 'certain substances'; but the expression is now so well known that its meaning is clear to every reader.

'Procuring' is short for 'procuring for immoral purposes' (i.e. prostitution). On its own the word simply means getting something or someone. Similarly, 'receiving' carries the unspoken or unwritten implication that it was stolen goods that were received. A 'receiver' may be one who receives stolen goods, or else a man who supervises the administration of bankruptcy proceedings. And there is the offence of 'dishonestly handling', i.e. stolen goods.

Not all stealing is dishonest. I was once telephoned by my Austrian aunt who informed me that I had been accused of musical theft by a writer in the *Daily Telegraph*. 'Fritz Spiegl' she read out to me over a long-distance telephone line, '*has stolen a march on the aleatoric composers of today* . . . You are a good boy,' she said. 'You wouldn't steal anyone else's march, would you?' And of course, one may also 'steal softly away' without committing an offence. 'When I was a boy' at school, wrote the seventeenth-century English poet Abraham Cowley, 'instead of ... playing with my fellows, I was wont to steal from them and walk into the fields.'

Simply 'taking' or 'taking away' (especially a motor vehicle) is also often used as an abbreviation. And 'joy-riding' is the most foolish word ever coined by news parrots. The proper term is 'car stealing'.

We all like to feel wanted, but not in the sense a 'wanted gunman' is. Is there an unwanted gunman?

'Initial investigations' by police may simply mean looking into it . . . provided they have 'something to go on' . . . 'Something to go on' must not be confused with 'having a go'. This is a term coined in the 1960s by a police chief who advised members of the public to tackle criminals and if possible arrest them. Once they do have 'something to go on', the policemen will move in to make an arrest. This is known in the papers as either 'pouncing' or 'swooping' – the latter suggesting a daringly Tarzan-like act, especially when done by 'Special Branch men'. In the *Guardian*, however, police once gloriously and inadvertently 'ponced'.

Neighbours suspicious: police find stolen copper

POLICE FIND CONSTABLE DRAWING IN ATTIC

Chinese police swoop on demo

Insp. J. Bates told the court at when arrested at the Royal Bucks Hospita! Mr. Downes kicked P.c. McLaughlin in the groin and broke his whistle chain.

Drugs swoop on jet

'Stripped' girl—Yard to probe

The two officers By Detective Constable Robert Bridgestock swooped on David Anderson. In his house, under (28),

The proposed film on Jesus Christ and sex: Mr. James Callaghan swooped in last weekend to condemn the idea outright, using a letter from a Tory M.P. as a basis for his action.

MAN HELD OVER FIRE

YOUTH HELD OVER GIRL'S BODY IN CASE

Japanese airline chief held in bribes case

26 musicians in smuggling case

Sikh girl wins trouser case

The Government is expected to change the rules on nurses' uniforms after a Sikh girl won

Move in drug case

8 HELD OVER LEAK

POLICE MOVE IN BOOK CASE

Managing director in drink case

MI5 steals march on secrets book

DETECTIVE STEALS THE LIMELIGHT

Detective Sergeant Wilf Marsden stole the limelight at the flower and vegetable

GAS RIG MEN GRILLED BY VILLAGERS

the thieves also broke into the police station and stole lead and copper piping, as well as all the china sanitary fittings. 'Said a puzzled inspector, 'We have nothing to go on ',

the bear was shot and killed with a 12-bore shotgun after a mile-long chase by zoo experts and police in Panda cars.

the young woman's dismembered body was found by police in three separate shallow graves at the edge of the golf course. She had not been interfered with.

After admitting hating unlawful sexual intercourse with a girl under the age of 16 on a day unknown between August 31, 1964, and March 1 this year. At Birkenhead Ralph

one policeman ...ng a diversion sign was not slow to grasp the importance of the situation. He said: " A hole has appeared in the road. Fife police are looking into it."

The magistrate. Mr St. John Harmsworth. referring to three other Biafrans similarly charged, said: " I cannot help feeling that if I try these other three cases, my mind is going to be coloured."

And when policewomen with the raiding party searched the woman who rented the house they found £32 in notes hidden in her brassiere.

The money, said Mr. John Quigin, prosecuting at Bedford, was part of a treasure chest the woman and her sister had built up.

A WEIGHTLIFTER from the Iriqi Olympic team was fined £100 at Marlborough Street today for shoplifting in the West End.

Miss Giavollela had pleaded guilty to stealing goods worth £25 from Tesco Supermarket: to assaulting a policewoman; and to dishonestly handling a garden gnome.

Policemen were pouncing in the nineteenth century too. The *Missouri Republican* on 12 February 1888 reported that one Inspector Byrnes had 'swooped down upon these lairs . . . that abound on Lower Broadway and New Street'. And in *The Pirates of Penzance* by Gilbert and Sullivan (1879), policemen pounce 'with cat-like tread'. Police also simply 'move'.

Having been swooped and pounced on, a suspect may be arrested. But before he is 'charged' (a word charged with a great many different meanings, from electricity to finance) his detention must be described in a neutral, non-committal way. Newspapers, after all, do not wish to suggest guilt before it is established, and possibly lay themselves open to actions for defamation. Their favourite word for 'arrested' is 'held'. At first it served only for headlines, but laziness soon brings such headline words into the text. 'Man held by Yard' is frequently seen — and would have given much amusement to earlier generations of Englishmen. 'Yard' was for centuries the euphemism for a penis.

More confusingly for modern readers, suspects may be held 'over' something; and 'over' is now often used in ways that uncomfortably suggest stronger geographical or literal connotations than abstract.

Once held, a suspect, especially one who is not quite so 'helpful' with police enquiries as the cliché suggests, will be questioned. The process is known in the press as either 'grilling' or 'quizzing', and is not confined by journalists to alleged miscreants.

'Grilling' at first meant torture by heat so as to extract a confession, but later came into figurative and sometimes facetious use: 'She comes today and shall be grilled', says George Meredith in a letter in 1894.

'Quizzing' is, according to tradition, the fanciful invention of one Daly, a Dublin theatre manager (and evidently something of a self-publicist) who in 1836 is said to have hired a band of men to scrawl the meaningless word 'quiz' on walls, so that it would be on everyone's lips. It now means questioning of a rather less determined manner than grilling. Newspapers like both words for their brevity and convenience, but use them interchangeably.

By the time investigations are complete (and they may be no more than an 'open and shut case') and the case comes before a judge, newspaper reporting takes on a different form. Judges' remarks are often reported verbatim, and so are the excuses or expressions of regret offered by the accused, or by lawyers on their behalf. Sentences given by the courts may range from the 'derisory' to the 'exemplary', or come in the form of a 'short sharp shock'. This is a relatively recent phrase coined by William (now Viscount) Whitelaw, as Home Secretary, when he was obliged to try to satisfy those who demanded 'exemplary' custodial sentences, while at the same time not filling the prisons to bursting-point. Hence his term, a 'short sharp shock', which he probably half-remembered from his days as an army officer: for in the British services the standard expression for brief but strong official disapproval is 'short sharp showers of shit'.

An A–Z of English News-write

ADAMANT From the Greek and Latin *adamas*, hard. A perfectly respectable word that is seldom used in everyday speech but over-used in media English, meaning firmness of purpose or obstinacy. People described as being 'adamant' in the press are likely to VOW← to do, or not do, something. The word also goes with reported denials. The Bible according to Fleet Street would report Christ's denial as: 'He was adamant he did not know the man.'

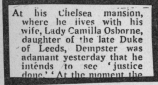

ALIVE AND WELL (AND LIVING AT) Newspaper English is full of apparently inseparable twin clichés. As that great journalist Rebecca West wrote in 1956, 'Journalism [is the] ability to meet the challenge of filling the space.' M&S TERMS←, as I have named such unheavenly twins in the following pages, help to meet that challenge faster – and avoid the need for thought.

MRS WORTHINGTON is alive and well and living near Basingstoke.

All 250 of her number turned up the other day, hoping to put sons as well as daughters on the stage in a new musical version of

For more information about Mrs Worthington, see **The Stately Homes of England** (page 24).

. . . AND THAT'S OFFICIAL A facetious tabloid addition to a statement based on information believed to be accurate, not hearsay. And that's fact.

APPEAL A request for help, or for reconsideration of a decision; also to please, attract, to be liked or loved, and therefore potentially misleading in headline use.

MAN WHO RECEIVED TROUSERS LOSES APPEAL

Hijack pilot's wife appeals to Heath

Mrs Castle appeals to railwaymen

AXES, CUTS AND CHOPS Often in the news: the words are conveniently short for headlines and appropriately sharp for text, with their expressive suggestion of violence. Unfortunately the mad axemen of Fleet Street do not know when verbal convenience-food turns emetic. 'Cuts' often demand the M&S← word 'swingeing' to accompany them – one of many newspaper words seldom encountered in speech. For other examples of metaphorical violence see HITTING. SLAMMING AND LASHING OUT←.

Crisp giant to axe 265 at Widnes factory

PEER 'AXED' FROM PARK COMMITTEE

The Tory peer, Viscount gleby, has been "aed" from the North Yorkshire Nati- Park Committee after 14 y

POLYTECHNICS THREATENED BY £80m AXE

About fifty students broke into the college, smashing a pane of glass and chanting: "No cuts, no cuts." A porter had his hand injured. The police

Big cuts to be made at hospital

Threat to axe teachers dropped

City primary schools face cuts axe

Grant axe will hit ratepayer

Hospital axe hits patients — doctor

DINNER LADIES TO GET CHOP

MISSILE FACES AXE

Ex-alderman dies

ONE OF EIGHT AXED BY TORIES

Jobs cut rocks brakes workers

The firm (Gillette Safety Razor Co.) were very happy to be associated in the effort to send the team to Sofia. Without their help we would have had to cut the team and this would have been a great disappointment to everyone."

Strike may cut meat in London

BACKING/BLESSING Projects that are officially 'blessed' may not receive official backing: thus 'blessing' means approval but 'backing' implies financial help.

BALANCED ON A KNIFE EDGE Five words of media padding to express one ordinary word: 'uncertain'. Also 'walking a tightrope', for another kind of 'balancing act'.

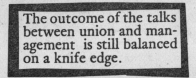

The outcome of the talks between union and management is still balanced on a knife edge.

BARRIERS Breaking through figurative barriers became popular after man first flew aeroplanes faster than the speed of sound, i.e. broke through the sound barrier. Such BREAKTHROUGHS← have now proliferated and there are no limits to the cliché barrier.

THE price of petrol is set to break through the 170p a gallon barrier.

KEITH CONNOR beat the pain barrier to take the European Championship triple jump gold medal in Athens last night.

BASIS A word that adds little bulk and less meaning but can sound grand. Thus 'on a global basis' merely means worldwide.

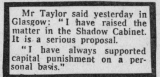

Mr Taylor said yesterday in Glasgow: "I have raised the matter in the Shadow Cabinet. It is a serious proposal.
"I have always supported capital punishment on a personal basis."

As for Mr Taylor of Glasgow, who supports capital punishment 'on a personal basis', does he mean he has ambitions to become a hangman?

BENDING OVER BACKWARDS Colloquial expression used to describe an eagerness or willingness to be helpful. Like many colloquialisms it must be used with care so as not to invite too literal an interpretation.

"The Home Office bends over backwards to help every serious sexual offender," Dr Field said.

BILLS, BILLS AND BILLS The word has many meanings: from a restaurant bill (now increasingly known by its American, inaccurate and confusing name 'check') to a bird's beak, a man's abbreviated name, an implement for pruning or cutting hedges and trees, a ceremonial weapon carried by eighteenth-century constables of the watch, a mattock or axe and a poster – especially one affixed by 'Bill Stickers', constantly under threat of prosecution.

Most frequently, when mentioned in newspapers, a bill is a piece of legislation put before, debated and perhaps passed into law by Parliament. When newsmen devise 'Bill' headlines they seem to forget all the other meanings.

Bill would let man marry his mother-in-law

Bill to alter rape laws

A rape Bill to overthrow a Law Lords' ruling was published said:

Mr Nixon revives old Bill

Cardinal attacks Bill

Cardinal H... ne, Archbishop of West-minster... the allied Roman shops... cansured with... leaders in con...

Tories give in on Bill

Caravan Club to object to Bill

Bill will bring joy to authors on the shelf

By Kenneth Gosling
Arts Reporter
News that a long-based pub... scheme would...

Little hope for brokers' Bill

The Insurance Brokers (Re

Attempt to sweeten Bill

Homosexual Bill goes to Lords

Homosexual Bill to get time

Bill attacks leap-frog pay claims

Government May Ease Bill's Passage

M.P.s cheer Bill on homosexual behaviour

Homosexual Bill to get time

Bill through

BITTER Stock headline word for stories about beer and the licensed trade in liquor, but 'mild' when the news is good.

Bitter row

by Jim Lynch

WHEN Liverpool's trading standards officers went out for a few "bevvies" they got bitter about the size of their "pint".

Now the controversy about whether a pint includes the gas and foam has come to a head again.

But while the weights and measures officers

might remain mild about the outcome the drinking regulars are likely to be angry over a survey which shows 93 per cent of Liverpool pubs and clubs are serving short measures.

The survey found the greatest deficiency to be an 11 per cent shortfall in a glass representing a loss of about 6p to the drinker. But the average was four

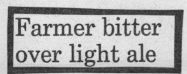

Farmer bitter over light ale

BLACK BOX The most common use of this term relates to the flight recorder carried by airliners, a device which, it is hoped, will in the event of a crash reveal information about the cause of the accident. It is in fact not black but bright yellow or orange, to make its recovery easier. The RAF used the term during the Second World War but did not invent it. 'Black box', denoting something intricate, potent or secretive contained in a plain, mysterious container, has been in use since 1933, when 'the Black Box Case' (as the press immediately dubbed it) was heard at Manchester Winter Assizes. It concerned fraudulent curative claims made for a mysterious piece of apparatus contained in a black box, and which had, of course, failed to effect the promised and paid-for cure. In the 1950s the Pye Record Company produced a gramophone which was named the Black Box; it was encased in a lacquered black wooden cabinet. For a short time the tachograph was called a 'black box' in newspapers, but this was soon driven out by the more dramatic SPY IN THE CAB←There appears to be no foundation for the claim occasionally heard that the flight recorder was invented by a Professor Black.

BLACK MONDAY (FRIDAY, etc.) A whole treatise could be written about black as the putative colour of the devil and all that is evil, or (as defined by the *OED*) 'foul, iniquitous, atrocious, horribly wicked, having dark or deadly purposes, malignant, pertaining to or involving death, deadly, baneful, disastrous, sinister'. The original Black Friday was the supposed Good Friday of Christ's crucifixion (what was good about it?); and Black Monday used to be the name given to Easter Monday. (On the Continent they have a 'Blue Monday' cliché where an Englishman might 'have that Monday morning feeling'.) The opprobrious use of 'black' is now frowned upon on grounds of racial harmony; and the National Union of Journalists has expressed its official intention of blacking the word 'blacking' in its strikes context (which is no bad thing when one reads about 'coal stocks at pitheads being blacked'). But it should be said that several African countries still cheerfully use the old Highway Code signs: 'Accident Black Spot'.

Britons accused of 'painting Uganda black'

Nairobi, Feb 16.—Radio Uganda today warned Britain to stop circulating what it termed baseless and unfounded propaganda. It also threatened

BLAZE Where ordinary people would investigate a fire, newsmen 'probe a blaze'. The next step upwards is an 'inferno'.

BLOWS, AND BODY BLOWS Blows are bad news; and body blows come from BOXING METAPHORS← — where they are rather less bad news than blows to the head. The 'body' element is added merely for makeweight in news stories; or for rhythm in spoken English.

Bus blow
–fares
go up
DEARER PETROL BLOW
Body blow to great white hopes
Ballot blow
A SHORTAGE of ballot papers has meant that
BLOW FOR MUSICIANS UNION
BLOW FOR LEYLAND BANDSMEN
Jobs blow
Blow for Liberals

BOGUS VERBATIM Manufactured quotations which put words or phrases into the mouths of people who never uttered them. Reporters do this either so as to make long and rambling replies more concise; or because they think everyone should speak in the style in which they write; or so as to give a certain slant to a story. Examples:

Question: 'Will you be seeing your wife while you are in England?'
Answer: 'No, I may not have time.'
Report: Smiled three-times-divorced Gary (56): 'I will not be seeing my estranged wife while I am in the UK.'

Question: 'Are you conducting in Manchester again, maestro?'
Answer: 'Not that I know of.'
Report: Scowled grim-faced music man Arthur Toscanono (87) as he flew out of Manchester's Airport yesterday: 'I will not be conducting Manchester's Hallé Orchestra again.'

BOTTLE Twentieth-century slang for courage, manliness, though its original application ('He's got no bottle') was a reference to quality rather than valour. The word was popularised in verbatim reports of the 1981 urban riots (being used by both police and rioters) and was given further currency in a series of television advertisements for milk, 'Gotta lotta bottle', which threatens to supersede the long-established PINTA←. Within a few days journalists appropriated it as a useful new cliché.

THE BOTTOM LINE American figurative cliché derived from the figure representing profit or loss in a statement of accounts, and meaning any important decision, judgement or conclusion; a fundamental or crucial point of fact; the heart of the matter.

£70 OFFER ON BOTTOM LINE

Advertisements appeared at the Hereford Jobcentre yesterday for 10 unemployed men willing to take their trousers off and be injected in their bottoms on a BBC Dick Emery television show.

dark. And yet the Labour Leader is surely right. If we are to go to open war with Parliament's full assent, then we must know the bottom lines of diplomacy. What, in short, we are going to war about.

BOWING OUT Resigning, or voluntarily leaving a job. It is one of many stilted archaisms used in Fleet Street, and suggests a person's ceremonious backward departure, possibly accompanied by a sweeping obeisance.

BOXING METAPHORS Although there are some well-loved and over-used cricketing clichés (no notable centenarian can reach his 'century' without being awarded the headline '100 not out') boxing metaphors probably are the commonest. From my 'ringside seat' I see every stage in, for example, wages bargaining described as a 'round', with or without the 'gloves off' (which may confuse the non-expert who thinks that gloves are put on before a fight, but the fighter knows that bare fists hurt more). Protagonists on either side may 'box clever' (a cliché not improved by the pseudo-genteel amendment 'cleverly'). At first, it may all be 'shadow boxing', with the occasional 'feint' – aimed 'below the belt' of the old 'sparring-partner', who is being used simply as a 'punch-bag'. And punches are a fruitful line: they may be fiercely 'packed' or tactfully 'pulled', or could turn into a deceptive 'sucker-punch'. And at that point may come the 'knock-out blow'. It will be the 'last round' when one side or the other 'drops its guard' and, 'punch-drunk', gets 'boxed into a corner' and, 'on the ropes', 'hits the canvas' to be 'out for the count'. At which point I 'throw in the towel' and hope to be 'saved by the bell'. However, I should add that the word 'stopped' has recently come into vogue as a euphemism for 'knocked out', perhaps in view of increasing criticism of this dangerous sport.

BREAKTHROUGH An alleged discovery or advance, as in:

KIDNEY OPERATIONS
BREAKTHROUGH

Most 'breakthroughs' appear to be reported in the 'quality' Sundays. This is not because Sunday papers have especially good medical or scientific reporters but because they have to be printed early: most of them are in fact on sale by Saturday evening. Which is why they are obliged to raid the previous week's medical and scientific journals and, by means of skilful rewriting, present days-old news as 'break-throughs'.

BRONZED AND FIT M&S TERM← for anyone returning from a holiday, even if he is carried from a plane on a stretcher.

BUFF An enthusiast for whatever is combined with this suffix. It comes from the American word for a person who likes to watch fires being put out by firemen: 'The Buffs are men and boys whose love of fires, fire-fighting and firemen is a predominant characteristic' (*New York Sun*, 1903) and got their nickname from the colour of the uniform worn by New York firemen. The Buffs in England were originally 'buff-coats', i.e. soldiers not in the once customary red and therefore not 'red-coats'. It now means one specific regiment of guards. 'In the buff' in Britain is a slang term for naked. See **Oh, What a Cover-up of the Bare Facts** (page 42).

TELEVISION has not been kind to us horror buffs. The last time I remember enjoying a shiver was with

Music buffs will probably tell you that it's not a genuine première and that the work was first performed on December 18, 1892. So it was, but that was a

WHEN MOVIE buffs get together they like to test each other's expertise with recondite quizzes. For example, "Which two leading men played opposite

Do-it-yourself buffs go into eulogies over Workmate and, according to Hickman, Black and Dekker, can't sell them fast

THE BULK OF Best avoided when there are connotations of weight or size in the context. Try 'most of'.

> The bulk of the participants in the Sponsored Slim weigh 13 stone or over. They hope to raise at least £1500 between them.

BUMP This is what things come down with when the aircraft industry, airlines, etc. are not FLYING HIGH←.

CANCER Like CRUCIFY←, SPASTIC← and other emotionally charged words, 'cancer' looks out of place in prosaic news reports. The intended allusion is probably to the tag, 'A cancer in the body politic', generally (wrongly) ascribed to Shakespeare, who used the word only once (preferring the English 'canker') and not in relation to politics.

> The milk surplus in Europe is a cancer in the middle of the EEC, said Mr Claude Villain. Director-General for Agriculture of the Eur

CARBON COPIES Real carbon copies are known as 'blacks' in newspaper offices. When journalists speak of 'carbon copies' they refer to events that show certain likenesses to each other, e.g. murder.

The dangers of smoking in bed were stressed by the North Merseyside Coroner, Mr. R. A. Lloyd, at two Waterloo inquests which he described as carbon copy cases.

Then the man went to the nightclub again and picked up another girl and committed an "almost carbon copy rape" said Mr Simon Hawksworth, prosecuting.

Man dies in carbon copy crash

CARD-CARRYING M&S TERM←. Just as the Christian is almost invariably said to be 'committed' and the homosexual PRACTISING←, so communists are always thought by media men to carry their membership cards with them wherever they go. British people don't make a habit of carrying identity documents, let alone party tickets.

(TO) CARPET To reprimand; formerly to 'walk the carpet', or to be 'called over the carpet'. The expression comes from servants being summoned to their masters' carpeted rooms, which were in notable contrast to their own bare quarters.

SIX MINISTRY MEN FACE CARPET OVER BLOODHOUND

MPs CARPET SCARGILL

CARROT AND STICK An M&S TERM← for inducement and punishment, respectively. The cliché is so much part of the language, especially of newspapers, that it is used mechanically and without thought of vegetables; and must confuse many a foreigner.

ON FRIDAY last your letters column carried a request that London Transport should woo car drivers by offering carrots.

London Transport's new promotion offering discounts on entertain---

CHARTER From the Latin word *carta*, a piece of paper; but of special significance for the Englishman ever since AD 1215, when King John agreed to the Magna Carta that guaranteed certain rights and liberties. The press has taken the event so much to heart that every pensions increase becomes a 'grannies' charter', unemployment benefit is a 'scroungers' charter', the allocation of allotments by the local council a 'gardeners' charter'; there are 'tea ladies' charters' and every other possible kind, including even a 'rapists' charter'. See also LICENCE TO←.

Nursery Schools: Mums Seek Toddlers' Charter

MP SEEKS WALKERS' CHARTER

Skivers' charter

Grannies' Charter

claims by ladies of similar occupation, and that he was not called upon to lay down a tea ladies' charter.

Tenants' Charter

Under the 1980 Housing more than 5 million tenants many new rights. The eight

THE TUC is prepared to set up a "Mrs Mopps" charter to combat low wages in the contract cleaning industry. It follows a report

CHIP ON THE SHOULDER He who wears this imaginary ornament harbours some kind of grievance, often combined with a sense of inferiority. I don't know how the expression came about, but a military origin is possible.

> **Rhyl Chef Told to Get Rid of "Chip on His Shoulder"**

CHOP AND CHANGE An M&S TERM← and usually a tautology. For an early use of the expression see HEART SWAP←.

> Police were complaining that many drivers on the M1 would chop and change lanes and make hazards for others.

CLASH An onomatopoeic word dating from about 1500, suggestive of the sounds of jousting – lance and spear on armour. The OED defines it beautifully: 'the loud sound of collision made by a heavy stroke or blow, the first impact of which is firm and hard, but is followed by a confused sound of many looser and lighter impacts', which would embrace both the sounds made by a pair of orchestral cymbals and the clatter of falling saucepans. Newspapers, however, use 'clash' figuratively for any kind of disagreement, however civilly conducted ('Mrs Thatcher clashed with Mr Kinnock in the Commons last night'), almost soundless collisions ('a clash of heads') or indeed any sporting meeting ('Liverpool clash with Arsenal next Saturday'). A useful headline-word but inadequate for telling a story.

CLAWBACK The Lord giveth, and the Lord taketh away . . . but the government gives, and then claws back what it can. An ugly neologism but an apt one.

> **Benefits clawback will be 1.5% below inflation**

COMMON-LAW WIFE See LOVE AND MARRIAGE IN FLEET STREET←.

CONFIRMED BACHELOR The unstated but implied suggestion that the man so described is homosexual.

COPYCATS Cats are proud, independent creatures and the idea that they slavishly imitate the actions of others is absurd. See also CARBON COPIES←.

Copycat shoplifter fails to prove point

Party clues to copycat attack

COPY-CAT young... who wanted to make a bomb after seeing "Spider-man" on TV may have been responsible for the theft of ....

CORNER SHOPS See HIGH STREET BANKS←.

COSTA . . . Columbus discovered the Caribbean coast on his last voyage in 1502 and called it Costa Rica, the 'rich coast'. The Costa Brava, Costa del Sol and other Spanish holiday places are favourite resorts with British holidaymakers and consequently often figure in newspaper reports. Journalists, with their unerring eye for a cliché, flog the 'costa' joke to death – 'Costa Topless', 'Costa Cuppa' and, of course, 'Costa Lotta'. One travel writer described a Spanish resort with a golf-course as 'Costa Golfa'. He must have been unaware that this means 'the whoring coast'. What the writer meant was 'Costa del Golf'.

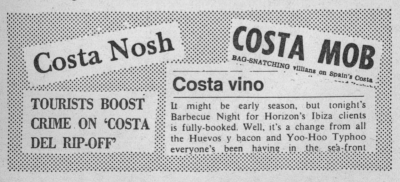

Costa Nosh

COSTA MOB
BAG-SNATCHING villians on Spain's Costa

TOURISTS BOOST CRIME ON 'COSTA DEL RIP-OFF'

Costa vino

It might be early season, but tonight's Barbecue Night for Horizon's Ibiza clients is fully-booked. Well, it's a change from all the Huevos y bacon and Yoo-Hoo Typhoo everyone's been having in the sea-front

CRACK A slang adjective meaning excellent, first-class. It is most often applied to rifle or pistol shooting ('a crack shot') but papers find it useful as a headline word in many other applications – even when the context might suggest a fissure. It was originally a country dialect word: an agricultural treatise of 1793 says, of Suffolk sheep, 'a crack flock, which is a provincial term for excellent'.

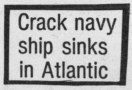

Crack navy
ship sinks
in Atlantic

CRITICAL 'Bishop critical', 'Actress improving': when newspapers report the condition of a sick or injured person they naturally tend to paraphrase what doctors or nurses tell them. But hurried or careless abbreviation (in both headlines and text) of statements like 'he is in a serious (or critical) condition' may suggest to the reader that it is the patient, not his condition, that is serious, critical or improving. A person in such an unfortunate position may well be critical of the persons or events that put him there – and he is not likely to be joking, or anything other than serious. American medical bulletins, always more verbose than English ones, tend to include phrases like 'He is in a stable condition.' The news cliché 'fighting for his life' is often absurdly and unthinkingly applied to any patient on the brink of death, even if he is a new-born baby. In reality an unfortunate man engaged in such a battle for life is probably unconscious or on a life-support machine, and in no condition to fight or battle for anything – although of course his body may be tenaciously clinging to life without his being aware of it, or anything else around him.

Roy Rogers, 66, singing cowboy star of many film and television westerns, was in stable condition yesterday after undergoing open heart surgery in hospital at Torrance.

VICTIM IS CRITICAL

BISHOP CRITICAL

WOMAN CRITICAL AFTER SHOOTING

4 critical after tinned salmon poisoning

both legs broken in the wreckage before firemen could free her. Last night, she was "serious" in hospital.

Actress Improving

Little David Jones was today fighting for his life after being born on Sunday three months prematurely. Doctors say he

CROPPING The practice of cutting down photographs so severely that little is left except the subject's eyes, nose and possibly mouth (as on the cover of this book). Why do they do it?

CROTCH, CRUTCH AND CRUNCH-SITUATIONS The 'crotch' is the area between the legs, where they join the trunk. A 'crutch' is a prop that supports the lame and helps them to walk. The two are related only insofar as a crotch (from French *croche*) was a fork in medieval English, and both came from the cross – Latin *crux, crucis* – albeit by different routes. Ancient doctors referred to a woman's 'intercrural parts' when they wanted to preserve politeness, and Urquhart, in his translation of Rabelais (1693), to an 'intercrural pudding' when he wanted to be lewd. 'Crunch' is an echoic word suggesting the kind of noise produced by some drastic action such as the sudden breaking of a bone. In its now over-used sense meaning a moment of decision, confrontation or decisive action, it was first memorably (if, for him, inelegantly) used by Winston Churchill about the Spanish Civil War: the 'outcome of the European crunch' (*Daily Telegraph*, 23 February 1939). Things have been coming to crunches ever since (except among some African leaders who appear to be convinced that they 'come to a crutch'); and 'crunch-situations' have not only proliferated but been joined by 'crunch-factors', 'crunch-points', 'crunch-days' and 'crunch-zones'.

CRUCIFY The word has a strong and very special meaning to many people but is nevertheless often used in an inappropriate context. The same goes for words like CANCER←, GERIATRIC←, and SPASTIC←. Journalists forget that many readers are offended by such an insensitive use of words.

The newspaper found itself crucified under a flood of letters from irate readers -

the 18 year old striker is now set to climb out from the £1m price tag that crucified him - unless he

CUPPA Media abbreviation for 'a cup of tea'. English tea-drinkers take their 'cuppa' with the help of a PINTA←. A 'cuppa char' has now lost currency but was once a standard newspaper cliché; from 'char', which was British army slang for tea, supposedly after some Indian word. Charwomen are much older, and are not 'tea-ladies'; see BOTTLE←, PINTA←.

DASH (noun) Any journey, however slow or leisurely, may be turned into a 'dash', especially in headline language. And when some small service is being rendered at the end of such a 'dash', it becomes a 'mercy dash' and the helper a SAMARITAN←. Hopes that fail to be 'raised' are said to be 'dashed' (see below).

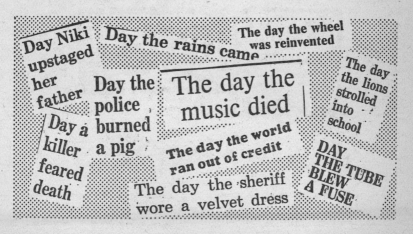

Skylab prize dash to San Francisco

. It also caused problems for Wonder Woman, Linda Carter, who was making a motorway dash for her concert at Liverpool's renovated Empire Theatre.

Concorde dash for Engelbert

From then on it was go for Mr Thornton. With the help of friends, a Perth radio station, and Qantas, he made the dash to San Francisco by car, Lear t, and commercial airliner.

DASH (verb) The Bible and Shakespeare are always a good guide for the use of words. Both use 'dash' literally and in a violent context ('Thou shalt dash them in pieces like a potter's vessel'), but Shakespeare once (in *Othello*) dashes spirits. Newspapers reserve the word almost exclusively for hopes – which either 'rise', 'fade' or are 'dashed'. The word gained initial popularity as a conveniently short headline word but soon entered text language. No journalist who failed to meet his girl-friend at an assignation would say to her, 'At seven my hopes were raised, by half-past they were fading and at eight they were dashed.' People do not say things like that, so why do they write them?

THE DAY . . . Stock opening for headlines. Thus, a total eclipse will be reported under the headline 'The day the sun died'; or a strike of transport workers as 'The day the country stood still'. The definite article is optional.

Day Niki upstaged her father / Day a killer feared death

Day the rains came

Day the police burned a pig

The day the wheel was reinvented

The day the music died

The day the lions strolled into school

The day the world ran out of credit

The day the sheriff wore a velvet dress

DAY THE TUBE BLEW A FUSE

DICING WITH DEATH News phrase for taking bodily risk.

> TEENAGERS have been dicing with death on Wirral's M53 motorway. Particular attention is being given by police to the highly dangerous game of "chicken" on the motorway.

> THREE men diced with death as they played an impromptu game of football with a live unexploded bomb.

DOG 'To dog . . . to follow doggedly, with persistence, closely in one's footsteps, possibly with hostile intent'. One is 'dogged' by misfortune or may, adjectivally, show 'dogged' determination. But it is the verb in its simple form that causes headline confusion. In London the word can also mean an abbreviation of the Isle of Dogs, by the River Thames.

> **Cutler approached over Dogs**
>
> A well-known but unnamed Swiss consortium is interested in developing the Isle of Dogs in London's Docklands, according to Greater London Council leader Sir Horace Cutler. He

> **'Hoodoo' dogs flying doctor's African planes**

> **Sabotage fear dogs North Sea**

> *INJURIES DOG LIONS*

> *AFRICA ARMS DOG PREMIER*

DOING A . . . Doing like . . . usually does, or is known for having done: a conversational colloquialism seen in headlines as well as text.

> **SIR MONTY MAY 'DO A MARSH'**
>
> By ROLAND GRIBBEN, Business Correspondent
>
> SIR MONTY FINNISTON, 63, is expected to be told shortly that the

> As news filtered through to Bradford about Edward Heath's latest murderous pat on the back for Mrs Thatcher, there was much happy speculation that he would do a Powell and urge his people to vote SDP.

DOWN MEMORY LANE The place where people are said to 'stroll', 'walk' or 'take a trip' when reviving old memories or revisiting old haunts. Probably from the title of a song by De Silva popular in the 1920s and 1930s.

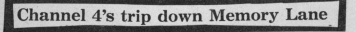

> **Channel 4's trip down Memory Lane**

DRAGGING FEET, SITTING BACK AND SHUTTING EYES Official inactivity, lethargy or dilatoriness. When the government is accused of dragging 'their' feet, in accordance with the plural confusions so rife in news prose the reader may wonder how many feet are involved.

Legal profession must not sit back

Pigeons: Council 'shutting its eyes'

thorpe community officer, now accuses relations Steel of dragging its feet British this review and breaking over spirit of the settlement. the

DRAMA 'A series of actions or course of events . . . leading to a final catastrophe or consummation' (*OED*). In the press almost any event may be elevated to drama status and may even become a SAGA←.

DRAWING A BLANK A gambling term made into a cliché and used to describe a fruitless line of enquiry. It is acceptable only so long as it isn't modified: drawing 'a series of blanks' immediately shows up the absurdity that lurks behind many a ready-made phrase.

DROPPING A BOMBSHELL The Fleet Street arsenal is a fearsome one. In around 1946 someone coined the imaginative term 'population explosion', probably as the postwar baby 'bulge' started to pop. By 1953 the American magazine *Time*, a publication not noted for reticence in adopting neologisms, still gave it quotation marks. But within a few years everything started to explode. The 'dog explosion', 'fast-food explosion', 'wages explosion', 'nursery explosion' – anything that could increase was said to have exploded. Unless, that is, things 'backfired', a disastrous thing that can happen when guns or cannon are fired (and a less dangerous one when a motor-car engine malfunctions). But now plans, engagements, reforms, announcements, proposals, etc. all 'backfire'. Prices 'rocket', and people get them: 'I had to give him a real rocket.' But if a woman of Chaucer's day had been given one, she would have worn it: 'There is no cloth sitteth bet[ter]', he wrote, 'on damiselle, than doth rocket.' John Evelyn, on the other hand, would have eaten it in 1693: 'Rocket is one of our Sallet Furnitures, which is sowne in the Spring.' As an outer garment worn by women, the rocket survived into the present century, and the herbal rocket (from Latin *erucca*) is still eaten – a kind of endive. Politicians issue 'broadsides', which are intended to make us think more of one of Nelson's ships than broadside ballads. 'Bombshells' are, for some inexplicable reason, always 'dropped', never fired – a curious, hybrid form of ordnance: for you *fire* shells but drop *bombs*. It all comes down to 'potential' (or

'political') 'dynamite', and may take all the political 'big guns' to defuse
the situation – or it could become a 'legal minefield'. Real bombs and
explosive devices are let off with such melancholy frequency that they
are abbreviated familiarly to 'devices' ('a device went off') – though
'making a bomb' is not always illegal. See also MINEFIELDS←.

ESTRANGED A good example of a Fleet Street archaism ('his estranged
wife') that is hardly ever encountered in everyday speech. It comes
from the old French estranger (now modernised to étranger).

EUROJARGON The European Economic Community has generated its
own euronews language. It is full of contrived **Acronyms** (page 32) like
'EMA', 'ERP', 'ERDF' and 'GATT'. The imaginary eurolandscape has
mountains made of butter, beef or skimmed milk, and lakes brimming
with wine; where roams a eurobeast called the Snake which lives on the
mythical Green Pound – most of the jargon totally incomprehensible to
newspaper readers. There are 'wars' over commodities like cod, lamb,
or fish in which not ammunition but floods of words and tons of paper
are expended. Pork has been officially reclassified as 'pig meat' and
flowers abolished. These are now 'non-edible vegetables'. 'Euro-' is the
standard prefix, and few of those who use it appear troubled by the fact
that it is homophonous with the medical 'uro-'. Perhaps one day
European urologists will hold a Euro-Urovision Song Contest.

EXTRAORDINAIRE For some reason writers often find it necessary to
lapse into French when writing about some person they consider in
some way extraordinary – a word in no way inferior for being English.

(TO) FACE To expect or confront. Not to be confused with 'facing up to', which means to expect something with courage and fortitude.

Lip workers face job cuts in new rescue operation

Shop stewards at Lip, the French watch-making concern, today demanded publicly that

TORIES FACE SPLIT OVER EUROPE

Channel pilots face cuts

Villa face cream of Italy

FACELIFT The popular name for cosmetic plastic surgery that removes wrinkles and 'lifts' the sagging face. But the word has now been annexed by the press for any kind of restoration, renewal, clean-up or alleged improvement, usually of buildings or places.

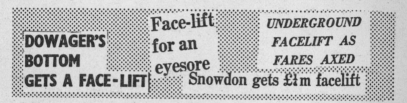

DOWAGER'S BOTTOM GETS A FACE-LIFT

Face-lift for an eyesore

UNDERGROUND FACELIFT AS FARES AXED

Snowdon gets £1m facelift

FACTS OF LIFE When I was young, knowing these meant one knew how babies were made. Today's facts of life are generally economic, political or in some other way harsh or unpleasant.

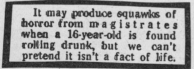

It may produce squawks of horror from magistrates when a 16-year-old is found rolling drunk, but we can't pretend it isn't a fact of life.

"The motor car is an accepted fact of life and people will continue to use their vehicles whatever the price of petrol."

FAMED Usually preferred by pressmen to 'famous'. It suggests a process, an artificial way of making someone famous, just as rice may be 'creamed'; and in the case of many famous, media-created 'personalities' the suggestion is apt. I wonder whether the children of journalists say to their father, 'Daddy, when I grow up I want to be famed like you.'

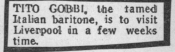

A specialist committee yesterday recommended to Parliament in New Dlhi that two coal-fired power plants at Agra be closed down in an effort to halt corrosion of the famed Taj Mahal.

TITO GOBBI, the famed Italian baritone, is to visit Liverpool in a few weeks time.

THE 'FAMOUS FIVE' CLICHÉ From a book by Enid Blyton and applied to any news story involving more than one protagonist, usually in a law suit. These have ranged from 'the Shrewsbury Two' to 'the Pentonville Six' and 'the Bradford Twelve'. Indeed, if the press were to describe in its own jargon the events leading to Christ's crucifixion the Apostles would doubtless have been called 'the Gethsemane Twelve'. When one of 'the Shrewsbury Two' was released the papers were in something of a quandary, but refrained from describing the survivor as 'the Shrewsbury One'.

SHREWSBURY TWO TO APPEAL

Paris three cannot be extradited

a London street. He also linked Quinn to a conspiracy to make explosives with five other men, four of whom were known as "the Balcombe Street Four."

'HANDLESS CORPSE' 7 TO APPEAL

PENTONVILLE SIX TRIAL SOON

TOXTETH 11 DEFENCE FUND

Bradford 12 verdict

FEAR TONIGHT STALKS THE STREET OF . . . Old-fashioned, overblown news phrase used for stories thought to warrant such treatment, as when, perhaps, a MASS MURDERER← is at large.

FIEND This word can reverse its meaning. In its normal sense (from various early medieval words, *feond*, *fond*, *feynd*, etc. – and modern German *Feind*) it means foe, enemy. But slang can give it a more favourable meaning, as in 'fresh-air fiend', 'music fiend', etc. (See also BUFF←.) When applied to a 100-year-old lady, as here, 'fiend' is quite absurd.

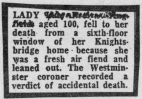

LADY ~~_____~~ *fiend* aged 100, fell to her death from a sixth-floor window of her Knightsbridge home because she was a fresh air fiend and leaned out. The Westminster coroner recorded a verdict of accidental death.

FLAK A German acronym for *Fliegerabwehrkanone* (*Flieger* = aeroplane, *Abwehr* = defence, *Kanone* = cannon – all one word in that accretory language), meaning anti-aircraft gun. It was coined by the Germans during the First World War and accepted into English soon afterwards (in RAF slang) with the same meaning. In peacetime it is used figuratively for any kind of opprobrium, blame or abuse, as in 'I'm having to take all the flak for someone else's mistake.' In this form, as an anglicised word, it should be written with a small 'f', but when a

German anti-aircraft gun or gunfire is meant, a capital 'F' is called for. The Americans wrongly spell the word with a 'c', possibly confusing it with the 'flack' = a press or publicity agent.

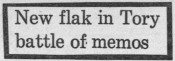

New flak in Tory
battle of memos

FLYING HIGH What the aircraft industry, airlines and anything connected with aviation do when things are going well. When things are less favourable, they 'come down to earth' (with or without a 'bump'.)

PLANEMAKERS FLYING HIGH WITH BRIMMING ORDER BOOKS

PLANEMAKERS' DOGFIGHT Why the stakes are sky-high

Down to earth with a bump

AIR hostessess with British Airways have been brought down to earth with a bump because they look 'scraggy.'

Flying high WEST GERMANY'S Lufthansa airline reported increased traffic revenue for the first half of this

Actress who is really flying high

FLYING INTO Reporters know better than most of us the long and tedious journeys between cities and the airports that serve them and bear their name. Airliners sometimes regrettably fly into mountains or other high objects but 'flying into London' (or most other cities) is possible only by helicopter. Besides, the dramatic present tense ('Russian Flies in from the Cold') can give rise to the verb/noun confusion so delightfully common in English news language. See also **Coming in from the cold**, page 24.

RUSSIAN FLIES IN
FROM THE COLD

FREEDOM FIGHTERS, TERRORISTS OR GUERRILLAS? As has become only too distressingly evident in recent years, the distinction between these is often difficult to make. Most revolutionaries and self-styled freedom fighters fight for the freedom to enslave others and claim the right to kill innocent people in order to achieve their aim. So what does the newsman do to appear impartial? If he works for the *Morning Star*, which draws most of its readership and revenue from interested parties abroad, he has no problem: all terrorists are freedom fighters, all policemen terrorists. The *Daily Telegraph*, on the other hand, applies the terrorist tag more freely, and generally with good reason. But the BBC, when referring to the perpetual fighting in Beirut, where some twenty different groups of Arabs have for many years been killing each other in the name of several kinds of 'freedom', has adopted the non-committal term 'fighter', as in 'PLO fighters today exploded a car bomb that killed six children.'

FUR AND FEATHERS FLY, IN FOWL PLAY This happens when there is even the smallest, gentlest or mildest disagreement among animal lovers. See also PURRFECT!←.

FOUL PLAY ON THE TURKEY FARMS

Feathers fly over sparrow shooting

Fur flies among the animal lovers

R.S.P.C.A. Fur and Feathers Fly

Feathers fly in egg trial

Feathers fly as birdland braces itself

THE row over the shooting of a sparrow in Lincolnshire country church took wing last night—with villagers planning a protest to the Bishop.

GERIATRIC As in 'This missile is now positively geriatric'— is a modern word. The *OED* did not have it before the 1972 supplement, because the general adjective for things to do with old age always was, and still is, 'gerontic' (from Greek *gerontos* = an old man). 'Geriatric', with the '-atric' suffix (*iatros* = doctor), denotes matters medical and came into popular use with the welfare state. So unless the treatment of old *and* sick people is described, the word 'geriatric' is best left to the doctor. See also CANCER←, SPASTIC←.

> **ALTHOUGH** one of the younger generation of missiles, this one is now positively geriatric.

GETTING OFF THE GROUND Derived from early attempts at flying, to suggest the idea of some scheme or project being launched in the face of difficulty or delay. But when it is used in such unsuitable applications as shown here, it is high time for 'grounding' it. See also FLYING HIGH←.

Councillor Sefton said he feared the motorway might never get off the ground if the opposition

...ALPA, the pilo. union, said that talks with the airline scheduled at the Department of Employment had failed to get off the ground.

AN ANTI-RAPE finally got off the ground in Liverpool yesterday despite earlier fears that it would fold through lack of interest.

GETTING (OR GIVING) THE GREEN LIGHT The traffic cliché. Unfortunately it breaks down as soon as it changes to a RED LIGHT←. There is no shortage of synonyms in English, from 'approval' and 'permission' to the less elegant but perfectly clear and unfussy 'getting the go-ahead'.

> ## Green light for the red light clean-up

GO In headline language, a usefully short word for resignation or dismissal from office, even shorter than QUIT←. When Ernest Marples was Secretary of State for Transport his reform of traffic laws incurred the displeasure of many motorists, who coined the slogan 'Marples must go'. In due course this appeared in thousands of car rear windows in the form of stickers. Others invented jocular variations on it, all of which the amiable Mr Marples collected and displayed in the lavatory of his house (including one that read 'Marples has been'). When Marples died in 1979, some motorists remembered him, and 'Marples has gone' stickers were seen.

WILSON GOES · Councillor had to go in a hurry · WHITELAW TO GO? · NOTT TO GO · PYM TO GO

GOING MISSING Until the middle of the twentieth century (including both world wars) unfortunate people were reported lost or missing. Now they 'go' missing. This is a German-based Americanism, from *verlorengegangen*, which perhaps also gave us the injunction 'get lost'!

He went missing on Sunday and his body was found two hours later in the River Ouse.

He went missing for over a week on the slopes of Anconcagua, the highest Andean peak, after setting out to say mass on the summit.

GRASS ROOTS These were originally non-political: the basic fundamentals of any concept, figuratively expressed. The first recorded political use (meaning the popular, rank-and-file support on which a party depends) dates from 1912, when an American senator said: 'This party comes from the grass roots. It has grown from the soil of the people's hard necessities.' In the same year Roosevelt's campaign was described as having come 'from the grass roots up'; and by 1920 one of the American parties used the phrase as a campaign slogan. Ever since then 'grass roots' have sprouted uncontrollably, especially in the British media. American commentators, being generally more inventive in their writings, have by now almost eradicated them, whereas British media parrots as well as politicians over-use such expressions *ad nauseam*. The American magazine *Newsweek* used an interesting variation in 1962 when commenting on Robert Kennedy's visit to the Far East: 'at rice-roots level' – without pausing to think that rice roots are permanently waterlogged. What is needed in the British press is a good dose of selective word-killer.

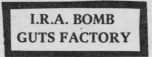

> ## Message from grassroots: it's getting worse
>
> He spent many years organising sport at grass-roots level - for which he received a
>
> Minister tastes grass roots politics in city
>
> ## Respect the grass roots, says Allaun

GUTTING The removal of the guts, or entrails, of an animal. In figurative media language, only buildings are gutted, usually by fire. Like many short English words, the third person singular must be treated with care if it is not to be confused with a plural noun.

> # I.R.A. BOMB
> # GUTS FACTORY

HANKY-PANKY Trickery, deceit. This word, with its jocular, jingling, juvenile reduplication, was used in the first volume of *Punch* as long ago as 1841, in a satirical mock court-case involving Lords Melbourne and Russell, and in which the former says to the latter: 'Oh! Johnny, this is your work – with your confounded hanky-panky.' It is probably a light-hearted adaptation of 'having a person at a good hank', which Grose (1823) defines 'to have made any contract . . . very advantageous to yourself' – in other words, a swindle. In modern newspaper usage 'hanky-panky' has conveniently unexplicit sexual undertones, as have HORSEPLAY←, KISS AND CUDDLE←, and 'slap and tickle'.

> # Hanky-panky gets left on the Barbed Wire

HEADACHES Anything from a minor nuisance to a major problem. Media headaches come only in large sizes, from 'king-size' to giant, and can affect any part of the anatomy except the head.

LIVERPOOL remained the headache as Liberal and Social Democrat leaders finally saw eye to eye last night over the shareout of seats for the next election.

Fitting 2,800 pages into a single volume was a bookbinder's headache. Random House said they were only able to do it because of the superior know-how of US paper and book manufacturing suppliers.

EVERTON'S emphatic 5-0 hammering of Luton Town has left manager Howard Kendall with a king-size headache.

Fleet faces air cover headache

manager said, 'Smith's knee is still a bit of a headache for me, but he'll be playing in a

BROADMOOR is as big a headache to the Department of Health, which inherited it 25 years ago from the Home Office, as it is to the people of Berkshire who live near it.

HEADS, BODIES, ARMS AND LEGS Many shades of meaning, from the anatomical to the figurative, and all manner of variations, are possible, from figureheads to WATCHDOG← bodies – with or without teeth.

Sun-Suit Schoolgirl Is Suspended By Head

HEADS HIT AT CUTS IN PLACES

HEAD SUSPENDED OVER GIRL

Heads back strike

Heads Strike Back

Travel to France on last legs

Arms are flown to Nigeria

At a meeting to discuss the route of a proposed ring road, the highways committee chairman said: "We intend to take the road through the cemetery —provided we can get permission from the various bodies concerned."

HEAD OF SWISS BANKING BODY SUSPENDED

INQUIRY OPENED

Backing for ear-rings row head

Pupils' hair length 'matter for heads'

TURKS HEAD FOR CYPRUS

New head for city race body

Rural body in urban office

WOUNDED HEAD FOR URUGUAY

By Our Buenos Aires S.

A British hospital ship ing British and Arge wounded from the battle in Falklands is due in Montevid

FOOT TO HEAD JOINT BODY

HEART SWAP The media word for heart transplant surgery. 'Swap' (or, equally correctly, 'swop') means an exchange, so the absurd implication is that the donor gets a diseased organ in exchange for his healthy one. But then, 'donor', from the Latin word for one who gives something of his own free will, is also preposterous, as the donor is (in the case of heart transplants at any rate) dead and in no condition to exert his will. 'Swap' sounds a modern, schoolboy sort of word, but is, in fact, of great antiquity. John Lyly (?1554–1606), in his *Mother Bombie* (1594), says: 'Ile not swap my father for all this.' 'Wife swapping', too, is older than we think: 'Wee, like two good Horse-corsers, made a choppe and change, and swapt vp a Rogeish bargain, and so he married my wife and I his,' wrote Robert Greene in 1592, in *Black Bookes Messenger*. Greene is described in the *Oxford Companion to English Literature* (1967 edition) as 'a witty Bohemian, of good intentions but poor performance, who drifted to a miserable end, and is said to have died of an illness brought on after a surfeit of pickled herrings and Rhenish wine'.

New heart swap at Papworth

A 44-YEAR-OLD West Midland man was given a new heart at Papworth Hospital near Cambridge yesterday. He is William Tromans, who has a French-born wife, Monique, and two sons, William (6), and David (4).

Father-to-son kidney swap

HELLO GIRLS Not an friendly exclamation but the tabloid name for female telephone operators, just as traffic wardens are 'meter maids'. 'Hello girls' must not be confused with call-girls.

HIGH STREET BANKS AND CORNER SHOPS 'High Street' and 'corner' have become almost obligatory prefixes for news items about commerce or finance. The implication that all banks, building-societies, even job-centres, are in the High Street and all small shops on street corners is foolish, absurd, and a good example of how newsmen can act like parrots. The original intention was, no doubt, to distinguish between merchant-banks and clearing-banks.

A CHILL wind is blowing through the High Street clothes shops. For the first time in recent years volume sales of clothing are generally down in the traditional

THE Government is considering closing the country's 672 High Street Jobcentres as part of its policy of public expenditure cuts. Savings could be more than £100 million a year.

STREET-CORNER tobacconists hope to make a killing (if that is the word) from the beleaguered state of their suppliers, the big cigarette

A SURVEY of mince bought in High Street shops has revealed large variations in the proportion of lean meat to fat—even

HITTING, SLAMMING AND LASHING OUT The Fleet Street words for expressing disapproval. The Pope and the entire College of Cardinals, as well as judges, doctors and the limbless, are apparently capable, when roused, of such violent actions. But to be 'hit' may also mean to be in some way adversely affected. By way of variation, verbal attacks may be 'unleashed', and of course there is the good old 'tongue lashing', an activity restricted to ant-eaters and newspaper writers.

SMITH HITS OUT AT TEBBIT

Mayor hits out

MP HITS OUT AT

Barristers hit out

Judge hits out

ANGRY HEATH LASHES TEDDY

Only a few weeks before, a Tory councillor was given a tongue lashing for opposing a vote to support strikers at a local electronics plant. He argued this would give *carte* ——he to mass picket violence

Widow of VC lashes the war grave ghouls

Black teacher lashes 'warning' to parents

ALTON LASHES THATCHER

THE VATICAN LASHES OUT AT CHARLES

Jenkins lashed by Owen

Fraser directors lash out at Lonrho

Councillor Carr hit out at the massive £21 million expansion plans for Liverpool Airport and he slammed the proposed multi million pound maritime museum in the south docks.

DOCKS CHIEF HITS OUT

LIMBLESS HIT OUT AT RISE IN LIVING COSTS

Angry Vicar hits at council

NW patients to be hit next week

Doctors hit out at pay review body

Star's broken leg hits box office

GUARDS' BAN SNOWBALLS —TRAINS HIT

JUDGE HITS AT PRESIDENTS IN MEMOIRS

Doctors hit at Minister

A PLAN to cut spending on road verge grass-cutting next year was slammed by West Lancashire County Council.

Travellers rap rise in fares

TORIES in Knowsley have slammed a twinning trip designed to show off borough's highspots to a group of visit German dignitaries ... because the

Thatcher policies slammed

HORROR A much devalued commodity in newspapers. For example, thirty-six people stranded for 'up to' two hours in a fairground vehicle, without danger or injury, are said to have experienced horror.

THE Bank Holiday weekend brought horror to 36 people enjoying the fun of the fair at Southport yesterday. They were left stranded 40ft in the air when a chair-lift ride suffered a power failure.

HORSEPLAY In Middleton's play *The Mayor of Queenborough* (1627) a character says: 'Fellows, you use no horse-play in my house.' He meant ordinary, rough and boisterous play, perhaps passing the bounds of prudence but no worse. Today, horseplay is one of the recognised sexually suggestive words in newsmen's vocabulary, together with KISS AND CUDDLE←. It comes from country talk: horses bite each other during mating – the male biting the female and the female the male. Newspaper 'horseplay' may also be found in reports of careless or over-excited but non-sexual behaviour that has perhaps led to tragedy.

HUMAN CHAIN Just as anyone murdering more than three people becomes a MASS MURDERER←, so more than three persons linking hands become a 'human chain'. And the inevitable description of any person unfortunate enough to be involved in a serious burning incident becomes a 'human torch'.

HURTLE From the French word *heurt*, a blow or clash, adopted into English in the late eighteenth century but now almost entirely confined to poetry or journalese overdramatisation, like PLUNGING AND PLUM-METING←, SOAR←, VOW← and dozens of others.

-IVE An often superfluous suffix used in words that do not require it. There is a rage for '-ives' at present, especially among the 'caring' professions and in the women's pages of the more radical newspapers and sociological journals, where husbands may range from the 'supportive' to the 'assaultive'.

In this country we have been living for the last 30 years or so under a very distortive tax regime. This has undoubtedly contri-

Mʀ DAVID BASNETT, general secretary of the disputive gasmen's union, must now be the man in England with the most tightly

The Minister for Transport said that reflective number-plates would in future be permissive.

magnified projections of the action inside studios to entertain the visitors to the new centre; larger studios for more participative broadcasts.

JOY RIDING One of the most foolish press euphemisms, meaning 'car stealing'. There is no joy in it when it ends in injury or death.

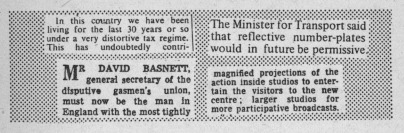

TWO good Samaritans unwittingly helped free a young joyrider from the wreckage of a stolen car yesterday. But the youth thanked one of his rescuers by kicking him — and then running away.

He left behind a written-

KEEPING A CLOSE EYE Looking at, or following, events very closely.

> Israel's Foreign Minister
> Moshe Dayan is said to
> be keeping a close eye
> on the situation. But it

KEEPING A FINGER ON THE PULSE Like A SHOT IN THE ARM←, is something better left to doctors or nurses.

> Constantly keeping his
> finger on the pulse of the
> industry, he believes that a
> matter of concern this year

KISS AND CUDDLE, KISS-AND-TELL Or 'kiss'n'cuddle' when used in headlines; a press euphemism for illicit sexual activity. One of the necessary qualifications for the description is that it takes place in some other place than in bed: perhaps in a car or the protagonists' place of work. The implication is always that the activity involved much more than just kissing and cuddling. During the 1960s there was a long court action which became known in the papers as the 'Kiss in Car Case' (and the couple involved, naturally, the 'Kiss in Car Couple'). The fact that there had been kissing in a parked car was never disputed; but the case hinged on establishing who had 'kissed' whom and on what part of the body. See also HANKY-PANKY← and HORSEPLAY←. After 'kiss and cuddle' may come 'kiss-and-tell' (or 'kiss'n'tell') – the revelations (probably induced by chequebook journalism) made by the former wives or girl-friends of the famous.

LAID OFF This is what happens to workers who are temporarily out of work because there is no work for them to do, as when, for example, their fellow workers are on strike. The expression comes from naval and military usage, where men are 'laid off' while their equipment may be 'laid up' or 'mothballed'.

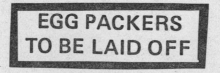

EGG PACKERS
TO BE LAID OFF

LAPSED CATHOLIC An M&S TERM←. Lapsed Catholics are probably former 'committed Christians', another M&S twin.

LATCHKEY CHILDREN 'You're twenty-one today, so you can have a latchkey to the front door.' 'Latchkey' is seldom heard in ordinary conversation. The normal word would be 'key'. But 'latchkey' survives as an archaism in 'latchkey children' – those who although young must be given a key to the house because the parents are out. By extension there are even 'latchkey dogs' – meaning dogs that are neglected and turned out on to the streets like children, not clever ones trained to unlock doors.

LEAGUE TABLES See TRACK RECORDS←.

LEAK An unoffical disclosure of information. There is also an 'inspired leak', which is semi-official, although 'off the record'.

No leak from Foot

LABOUR COUNCILLORS ACCUSED OF LEAK ON HOMES REPORT

LETTERS A fancy word for literature, anglicised from the French *homme de lettres*, 'man of letters'. To be used with care, for fear of misunderstanding.

> is not useless; it gives a clear summary of the events of Colette's life and the stages of her literary production, and contains some valid judgments on her art.
> Its weakness, if any, lies in a certain naïveté of phrasing in dealing with "the great lady of French letters". Miss Marks sometimes sounds

LIBBERS AND LIBERATORS Liberty has been a battle cry since the eighteenth century, when the French Revolution hopefully proclaimed freedom, equality and brotherhood. But, of course, it depends who is 'liberating' whom or what. The Russian liberation of Afghanistan? The American liberation of Vietnam? Or indeed the euphemism, 'I liberated it', with which allied soldiers of the Second World War would describe some object they had looted? 'Liberation fronts' and 'liberation organisations' have proliferated in the last decade or two, with additional parrot-phrases such as 'self-determination', FREEDOM FIGHTERS←, etc. The organisations' names are always devised with a good acronym in mind (see page 33), their causes certain to produce bloodshed and tyranny as great as, if not greater than, the regime from which they seek to be liberated. Any and every cause worthy of someone's attention, whether it be factory-farming, egg production or sex equality, has been elevated to a cause for 'liberation', coupled to the inevitable abbreviation 'lib' which, in turn, is extended to 'libbers'. But one thing is certain. Whoever coined the term 'women's lib' should first have consulted a good dictionary: 'lib' (from Old English, *lybban*), to geld, castrate; and 'libbers', the men who travelled the country castrating pigs so that these would grow fatter and produce better pork. In Sir William Davenant's play of 1649, *Love and Honour*, occurs the line, 'Sure he is libb'd; he hath certainly no masculine business about him.' Women's libbers now prefer to be described as 'feminist', but the adjective should not be confused with 'feminine': the two qualities are not always found in the same female person.

LICENCE TO Headline adaptation of the book title *Licence to Kill*. See also **The Stately Homes of England** (page 24) and CHARTER←.

LICK In the sense of beating or defeating someone or something, this has been informally used in English since the middle of the sixteenth century, defined in a book of 1567 as 'Lycke – to beate' . . . long enough, one would have thought, to make writers pause and consider the other meaning of the word.

Their range of packaged furniture licks all the others into a cocked hat. Customers, he adds, come back and buy more.

Our women lick male sportsmen

NOBODY but a millionaire can afford to have arthritis," says Dr O. C. Wenger, the famed doctor, who licked venereal disease in the army during World War II.

LIFE SAVINGS Any sum in excess of about £50 taken by thieves from a poor person is automatically described in the press as 'life savings'.

LIKE A HOLE IN THE HEAD As in 'I need a car like I need hole in the head', which means 'Not at all, on the contrary, I would hate to have a car.' Comes from a Jewish (and now American) saying and is common in fashionable journalism.

> When he joined Collins, his present publishers, he was told that they needed another thriller writer like they needed a hole in the head, and someone went so

LOOM Only unpleasant things 'loom'. The word comes from sailors' slang for an object, ship, etc., coming slowly and indistinctly into view, perhaps on the horizon, but not necessarily spelling danger.

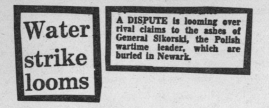

Water strike looms

A DISPUTE is looming over rival claims to the ashes of General Sikorski, the Polish wartime leader, which are buried in Newark.

LOVE AND MARRIAGE IN FLEET STREET Tabloids and heavies tend to treat the subject differently, although much of the vocabulary is common to all newspapers. Innuendo is rife: for example, a woman's lover may be coyly described as 'the man in her life' or 'constant companion'. But descriptions of relationships are becoming ever franker. Until recently it would have been considered actionable for a newspaper to refer to a man's woman-friend as his 'mistress', but not if she was described as his 'house-guest' or 'live-in'. The place they occupy together, if unmarried, is their 'love-nest', and if a child springs from such a union it is called a 'love-child' – thereby suggesting that children conceived in wedlock are never the result of any loving act. Yet in spite of increasingly liberal views on cohabitation, writers are often extremely coy about giving factual descriptions of the true status or relationship of or with their loved and loving partners. And some women writers are so embarrassed about it all as to take temporary leave of their spelling and grammar: 'My feller' or 'the man wot I live with'. Why not 'concubine'? Or 'cohabitant', which has the advantage of dual gender? Or the charming old English word 'fere' ('a companion or partner, whether male of female')? In the north of England one still occasionally hears 'living over the brush', from the old gipsy custom of declaring a couple married if they ceremonially stepped over a broom (= 'brush' in the north). Americans have gone to absurd lengths of invention: 'posselcue', an acronym loosely derived from 'person of the opposite sex sharing living-quarters'; 'mingles' (compounded of 'mixed singles'); 'apartmate'; 'symbiotic mate'; or 'my biological companion'. 'Common-law wife' (or more rarely husband) is a euphemism now often seen in newspaper reports, even of law suits, meaning partners in a relationship thought to have some duration or stability; and is increasingly copied by people in everyday conversation. The condition is certainly common but there is nothing lawful about it. A common-law wife may – and should – have certain rights, but she is not a wife and there is nothing in English common law to make her into one. Only Scottish law recognises unions of 'habit and repute' but even it has no power to legalise an unlawful union. See also **The Fleet Street Ages of Man** (page 13) for 'boy-friends' and 'girl-friends'.

LUBIANKA Name of the most notorious prison in Moscow. Facetiously applied to big, anonymous buildings, especially those housing rival newspapers; or ugly grey examples of modern architecture.

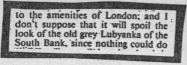

to the amenities of London; and I don't suppose that it will spoil the look of the old grey Lubyanka of the South Bank, since nothing could do

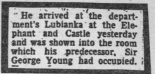

He arrived at the department's Lubianka at the Elephant and Castle yesterday and was shown into the room which his predecessor, Sir George Young had occupied.

M&S TERMS The British have always shown a fondness for commercial partnerships; and the names of old-established firms, some long-forgotten, are almost part of the language:

A *Sewell & Cross* young man, a *Howell & James* young man,
A pushing young particle, 'What's the next article?'
Waterloo House young man.

W. S. Gilbert, HMS Pinafore

'Dickins & Jones', Swears & Wells', 'Fortnum & Mason', and even 'The Bourne from which no Hollingsworth returns', etc. Curiously enough in popular speech the second partner is often omitted, and people speak (or in some cases, alas, spoke) of 'Fortnums', 'Swears' or 'Bournes'. Only 'Marks & Spencer (also affectionately known as 'Marks & Sparks') seem to be immune from the dangers of take-overs or closure. I have therefore borrowed their name to describe those newspaper terms which appear apt only when used together: see ALIVE AND WELL← and subsequent examples.

MASS MURDERER A man who has murdered two persons is a 'double murderer', a killer of three a 'triple murderer'. But anyone with four or more victims becomes a 'mass murderer' (or 'killer'), when referred to in a newspaper. A *bigamist* is a man who illegally marries another woman while still married to one previous wife. If he takes more 'wives' he should strictly be called a *polygamist*.

MILD See BITTER←.

MILESTONES Like CARBON COPY← crimes, 'milestones' are a newspaper archaism. When did you last see (or rely on) a milestone, or even hail one?

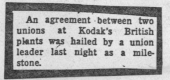

An agreement between two unions at Kodak's British plants was hailed by a union leader last night as a milestone.

MINEFIELDS These are figurative, either political or legal, and probably also 'potential dynamite'. See DROPPING A BOMBSHELL←.

MOST WANTED MAN Superlative applied to an alleged criminal sought by the police. There is, however, no comparative degree of desirability, and if two criminals are on the run at the same time, then *both* are most wanted rather than one of them the 'second most wanted man' in Britain.

MOUNTING PROBLEMS M&S TERMS←. In newspapers there are no ordinary problems: they are either 'mounting', or 'grave'.

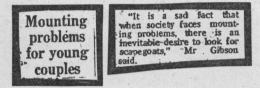

MOVE The threat or promise of imminent action; at first a headline word, but later adopted into general news language.

MUNCHING, QUAFFING, TUCKING INTO AND WASHING DOWN 'Eate softly, and drinke manerly, take heede you doe not quaffe', says a book of 1577 on the subject of table manners. Although most people heed such advice in everyday life, in the press they are invariably depicted as gross and greedy consumers of food and drink. They do not eat their food but 'tuck into it' and (like horses) noisily 'munch' it. They 'wash it down with a 1966 claret' – or whatever is their 'favourite tipple'; and however grand and delicate the vintage, they do not drink but 'quaff' it. Such swilling, quaffing, chewing (and probably simultaneous talking with wide open mouth) are surely seldom seen outside television drama studios, where this kind of behaviour is an everyday cliché. Tea, in newspapers, is never drunk but 'sipped'; cigars not smoked but 'puffed'. The whole range of parrot phrases is usually introduced by another couple of obligatory images: '*(Champagne) corks popped*, as the mayor and guests *sat down to a slap-up banquet.*' I like to imagine a conversation at the bar of El Vinos that goes something like this:

'Hello, Jack. Like a drink?'

'No thanks, I'm already quaffing, but I could munch a cheese roll. But why aren't you washing down yours with your favourite tipple?'

'To tell you the truth, I'm on the waggon, so I'm just sipping a coffee . . . Trouble is, every time I sip a coffee I seem to need to puff one of my favourite smokes.'

Away from the fleshpots of the City yesterday my man sampled a salad of weeds in the mountains of Powys in mid-Wales.

He tucked into a plate of hedgerow plants untouched by chemicals during the National Centre for Alternative Technology's open day at Machynlleth.

Councillor John, Labour leader of W shire County Counc the proof of the pud in the eating yesterday when he learned that he did not really take his life in his hands when he tucked into a protest rhubarb pie.

The rescued men shivered in their borrowed clothes and sipped tea from thick and chipped tin mugs overnight.

FRESHLY-SCRUBBED Argentine prisoners of war tucked hungrily into a hot breakfast of sausages and baked potatoes yesterday as they sailed for home on the Canberra.

A new recruit, a former baker, surprised the pals with a gift of 60 home-made biscuits. The richly-flavoured delicacies were soon gone, washed down with plenty of beer and wine.

By the hosts own reckoning, there were at least 25 grand slam title holders tucking into their sausage, bacon and eggs, and eight Wimbledon champions of the female persuasion. Mr Tinl—

Corks' pop as the superstars' fly in

him and his wife — chicken soup, roast lamb apple pie, washed down with German wine — night

CHAMPAGNE corks will be popping at Liverpool's Royal Court theatre to-night to celebrate

—Dr Pierre Bastien tucking into mushrooms.

we eat out, is tomato soup, rump steak with chips and peas. followed by Black Forest Gateau, washed down with the house wine.

Champagne corks popped last night as over a hundred guests sat down last night to a slap-up dinner

★ The trouble is Arthur's just too slim for the roly-poly panto part. So little Claire's making sure the friar tucks in to those goodies.

MYSTERY SUB This invariably means a Russian submarine on a spying mission.

NEGRO A generation ago the normal, accepted and inoffensive word for a person of brown skin and African ethnic type. There were also the euphemisms 'coloured' or 'of darker hue'; but all such have now joined the offensive 'nigger' on the list of taboo terms. People have been reduced to 'black' and 'white'; and Negroes call themselves 'black' with more pride than accuracy: I have never seen a *black* man – and if I ever saw a *white* one I would call for a doctor. The change can be traced to the famous 'Black is Beautiful' speech made by Martin Luther King in 1967, when he also launched a poster campaign with that slogan.

NIGHTMARES Fleet Street persons seem to suffer much from disturbed sleep: any slight inconvenience or trouble is likely to be elevated into a nightmare.

£8,500 FOR NIGHTMARE

NIGHTMARE DRIVE TO THE SHOPS

'Nightmare' search for good pub food

NO WAY! As a negative exclamation, refusal or denial, this comes to us from the German *keineswegs* in an American-English translation. Not to be confused with the established usage, as in 'I am in no way responsible', or 'There is no way for pedestrians here.'

> Hundreds of spectators were stunned as 5ft 2ins Michele leaped from her seat, shouting "No way", when her rival's name was announced.
>
> She lunged at the new Miss Vauxhall, 20-year-old

OF MANY YEARS' STANDING 'For many years' is usually better, especially when, as in this instance, the writer was concerned not with standing.

> As one of the seven who sat down through the playing of the National Anthem at the North Islington Labour Party dinner last year, may I make a few points on your article of March 7.
>
> Firstly, in spite of being a republican of many years standing. this was the first time I have ever been " admonished " for it—to date Willie Hamilton

. . . OF THE YEAR An invention of the publicity industry ('Pipeman of the Year', 'Whisky Expert of the Year', 'Margarine Cook of the Year', etc.). Newspapers and the rest of the media dutifully publicise this kind of rubbish, which is, of course, meaningless and as easy to fake with fraudulent 'votes' as the way pop industry for years falsified its 'charts'. *Everybody* is somebody's Man, Woman or Child of the Year.

A collage of newspaper clippings:

GEORGE IS 'BASSOONIST OF THE YEAR — ...b Reynolds is Young Computer Brain of the Year, ... George Reid, the new Shepherd of the year. Photographer of the Year, Mrs Lola Clark ... **'CAR OF THE YEAR'** ...d become your ... Try this ... own Cook of the Year Alan h husband's very own ... declared Neighbourhood Young Policeman of the Year. He is now about to ... The award of the BBC Moneybox Unit Trust Investor of the Year has been won by a ... In 1981 I was declared Young Musician of the Year by Scunthorpe Amateur Music ... And we are proud to perpetrate what is undoubtedly the ...in Offer of the Year **Cartoonist of the Year** and cheques to Jonathan Steele, International Reporter of the Year, David Hencke, Specialist Writer of the Year, and Posy Simmonds, Cartoonist of the Year. And we are proud to ... what is undoubtedly the **BARGAIN OFFER OF THE YEAR** with free subscription to the paper

...was concerned over an injury to last season's Robinson's Barley Water Young Player of the Year, Ronnie Whelan. ...yesterday she was named Top Secretary of the Year by the London Chamber of Com... and Ind... **AUDI 100 'CAR OF THE YEAR'** A Composer of the Year competition was launched yesterday by Barclaycard, in association with Nene ... Northampton ... Ricky Skaggs, 28, who had a meteoric rise to fame as a traditional country singer, was named Male Vocalist of the Year on Monday night at the Grand Ole ...ries **Young Musician of the Year** In this PROFESSOR IS sole represent MANCUNIAN OF Northern Engl... **THE YEAR'** the Pop Pianist of the Year ...of the Year competition.

OFFERS OF CASH always 'pour in'. There is no other way for cash to arrive when reported in newspapers.

(TO ACT) ON A HUNCH An action taken in response to an instinctive feeling rather than reasoning; guesswork.

OLÉ See OO-LA-LA!

ON THE JOB To be used with care: a vulgar euphemism for copulation.

> **MOTHERHOOD.** — About 65 per cent of women who worked before giving birth were back on the job a year later, a survey conducted by Tel Aviv University found.

OO-LA-LA! Tabloid writers' Frenchifying cliché. They also think Spaniards go round all day saying 'Olé!'

OPERATION——— A legacy from the Second World War, when military operations were given code-names for the sake of secrecy: Operation Mulberry, Operation Sealion, Operation Pluto, etc. Journalists like to dramatise humdrum news by calling, for example, the arrival of three roadsweepers 'Operation Clean-up'.

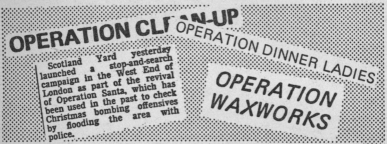

OPERATION CLEAN-UP

Scotland Yard yesterday launched a stop-and-search campaign in the West End of London as part of the revival of Operation Santa, which has been used in the past to check Christmas bombing offensives by flooding the area with police.

OPERATION DINNER LADIES

OPERATION WAXWORKS

ORGANS Musical instruments; what the Scots call 'a kist o' whistles' (i.e. chest, box, of pipes). One of those words that should carry perpetual danger-flags; for it is also a euphemistic abbreviation of 'sexual organ'. The *OED*, risking further confusion, gives as one of its definitions, 'A means of action or operation, an instrument, a "tool"'; and also 'an instrument, medium or means of communication, or expression of opinion; specially applied to a newspaper or journal'. To call a paper a 'party organ' is to suggest unquestioning allegiance to a certain cause. Political spokesmen are sometimes referred to as 'mouthpieces'.

ORGAN TROPHY
LOST BY INCHES

GIRL'S STOOL HIGH

From Our Special Correspondent
BLACKPOOL, Tuesday.

A girl, only 5ft. 2in. tall, lost the Edwin Coppock organ solo trophy by three points at the competitive musical festival here to-day. She found too late that the player's stool was adjustable to bring the stops and the pedals within her reach.

OUR HANDS ARE TIED An overworked cliché heralding what is usually a lame excuse.

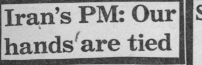

Iran's PM: Our hands are tied

SEX EDUCATION
Parents say their Hands are Tied

OVER (1) Journalese for 'more than', as in 'he waited over ten days'.

OVER (2) The over-use of 'over', both in headlines and text (as well as everyday speech), is a comparatively recent habit. The trouble with 'over' is that its geographical connotations are too strong to allow a comfortable figurative, abstract use. But as newspapers provide the staple reading matter for most of us – and newspapermen often go into broadcasting and television, bringing their bad habits with them – 'over', like other news clichés, has become common in spoken English. One now hears expressions like 'I warned him over not eating his lunch', 'He was fined over speeding' and 'She was feeling chuffed (i.e. pleased) over her promotion.' The final line in the BBC radio soap-opera, *Mrs Dale's Diary*, 'I'm worried about Jim', would now be changed to 'I'm worried over Jim.' When newspapers reported some disturbances in Portugal about the exhumation and reburial of a former state president, a headline read 'Riot over the head of late dictator'. Thus is the language impoverished by the media. What about 'on', 'about', 'after', 'for', 'in', 'with', etc.?

OVERLY As an adverb 'overly' is inferior to 'over', in the sense of 'excessively', as in 'overly anxious'. It is an American invention, although some Scottish speakers followed this unattractive usage before the Americans made it fashionable. Critics seem now to be overly fond of it. If there were no other reason for avoiding it, the possibility of confusion by misprint with 'overtly' would be enough. (However, 'overly' was once a perfectly normal English adjective, meaning overbearing, supercilious, slighting, etc.)

and a supporting cast that looks as if it's been disowned by Federico Fellini as overly grotesque. But after all play up to the hilt. se ten. But you need not be overly sensitive to conclude that there must be something odd about the book, something sufficient to upset

'I suppose one of the reasons why we are not overly impressed about what we have is because we feel cure about it. It's not as

OVERWHELMING (As in 'the overwhelming majority'.) A needless inflation and intensification of what can be expressed more forcefully with simpler words like 'big', 'great', 'large' or even 'vast'. The meaning of the verb 'to whelm' is to overturn, capsize, or even to turn over: a gardener would 'whelm' the soil with each spadeful as he dug his garden. Also, therefore, and by extension, it means to bury completely with solid matter, or submerge with liquid. There may even be some wartime echoes in the usage, for in times of armed conflict one hears of troops of one side being overwhelmed by their foes. But as so often happens, over-use can destroy the most imaginative phrase. Each time I hear or read statements like this one, I find myself more and more underwhelmed.

The police and prison services who came into contact with Rastafarians needed to know the official policy towards them, Mr Thomas Cox (Wandsworth, Tooting, Lab) said, when he opened a short debate on the attitude of the police and prison authorities to Rastafarians.

Following the events in Brixton last week this debate was appropriate.

Few people seemed to understand that to these youngsters, who were overwhelmingly black, this was their belief and their religion. At a time when

PET 'An animal which is indulged and fondled and which returns the love given to it, with faithful devotion' – but this definition is not wide enough for Fleet Street, where even a bloodthirsty alsatian dog which has just devoured a family's baby qualifies for the description of 'pet'. When a group of football spectators on their way to Anfield for a Liverpool v. Manchester United match chased away a dog that was threatening to bite a child, the local paper carried the news under the headline 'Reds Supporters Rescue Toddler from Dog Attack'. The Manchester papers said, 'Liverpool Hooligans Attack Child's Pet'.

THE baby son of England soccer star Alan Devonshire has been savaged by the family's pet alsatian.

Pet Elephant Tramples Six

PETTICOAT A headline word indicating the presence of women; and an archaism, since one now seldom hears the word, which has been superseded by 'slip', or 'underskirt'.

Petticoat pickets stay defiant

PINPOINTING/HIGHLIGHTING What usually happens to a PROBLEM←.

DANGER SALMON TINS PINPOINTED

PINTA A facetious measurement of milk which looks like surviving repeated decimalisation attempts. It is, of course, short for 'a pint of milk' and was invented in the 1950s for an advertising campaign with the slogan 'Drinka pinta milka day'. Pinta can now be heard even from the lips of staid BBC announcers without so much as a hint of irony. Part of the contents of a pinta may find its way into a CUPPA←. When decimalisation prevails in Britain we may get the 'litra'. See also BOTTLE←.

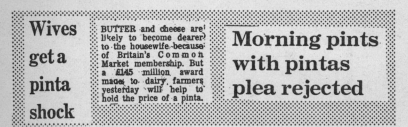

Wives get a pinta shock

BUTTER and cheese are likely to become dearer to the housewife because of Britain's Common Market membership. But a £145 million award made to dairy farmers yesterday will help to hold the price of a pinta.

Morning pints with pintas plea rejected

PIPELINE An imaginary duct through which newsmen pass things solid, liquid and abstract.

A LIFELINE plan for three doomed tower blocks in Birkenhead could be in the pipeline. Carol, Havelock and _____ Road have been marked

PITCHED BATTLE In its strict sense, a 'pitched' battle is one in which opponents fight from prepared and defined territorial fields or positions: an archaic kind of military operation suggestive of rows of redcoats facing equally carefully placed enemy forces. But in modern news use, the word 'pitched' is added merely as a makeweight, to balance a headline or give a desired rhythm to speech. M&S TERM←.

PITCHED BATTLES IN EL SALVADOR

A 25-years-old bachelor was stabbed to death in a pitched street battle in South London to-day.

PLAYING A WAITING GAME A journalistic sport, like TRACK RECORDS AND LEAGUE TABLES←.

through a loud-hailer. A standard police operation in such situations was put into operation, with the object of "bottling up" the two men and playing a waiting game in the hope of talking them out.

The police are playing a waiting game, having abandoned hope of catching the lad during his frequent

PLUMPING AND OPTING 'Plump': 'Of full and rounded form: having the skin well filled or elastically distended; sufficiently fleshy or fat to show no angularity of outline; chubby'. These are some definitions of this adjective, which comes from the middle Dutch *plomp*, carrying the same meaning (though modern Dutch now uses the word in the sense of clumsy, ungainly). 'Plumping', in the sense of an emphatic choice (probably from French *plomb*, a piece of lead) is used as in 'falling for' something. 'Opting' means much the same, and comes from the Latin *optare*, to choose, *optionem*, choosing, probably related to 'optimum', the best, since one would be expected to make the best choice available. Options have acquired a great vogue in recent years, to the almost total exclusion of choices.

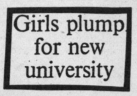

Girls plump
for new
university

PLUNGING AND PLUMMETING Journalese words for 'falling' and not generally used outside newspapers. They are thought to add drama to a story, as when the first issue of the *Daily Star* led with a report of a model who 'plunged' from a window. Rival papers quickly pointed out that the plunge had been all of three feet, as the window was on the ground floor. 'Plummeting' comes from an old French word *plommet*, a ball of lead, which also gave us plumb lines and plumbers (see above). There are also less dramatic plunges, as when the value of the pound drops (or 'slides'); and on the women's pages necklines may plunge.

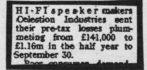

HI-FI speaker makers
Celestion Industries sent
their pre-tax losses plummeting from £141,000 to
£1.16m in the half year to
September 30.
Poor consumer demand

POLITICAL FOOTBALL A favourite media game, or 'ballgame'; political footballs are generally used by those who themselves complain of being kicked around. Like 'political' or 'potential dynamite', a common M&S TERM←.

Railways since nationalisation have been used as a political football to be kicked around according to the party whim without regard to the public.

We are united and determined that from now on that blacks in England shall be treated on a simple basis of merit and ability and that we shall no longer be political or sociological footballs.

POWER Vogue suffix of the militant 1970s and 80s, which can have almost any word stuck in front of it to describe a fashionable pressure group. It sprang from the cry of militant Negroes, 'Black Power!', which was coined in June 1966 by a Mississippi student, Stokely Carmichael, but William Safire suggests that Carmichael was only sloganising what had in fact been merely a simple statement made a few days earlier by a black congressman, Adam Clayton Powell, who used the two words conversationally rather than emotionally. At first, 'black power' meant power *shared* with whites ('not anti-black but anti-anti-black', as was said at the time) but militant groups like the Black Muslims and Black Panthers soon turned a sensible statement into a warcry. The cliché has since been adopted by publicity-seekers for many fashionable issues: toddler power, animal power, women's power, vegetarian power, etc. It may be mentioned that in the 1982 Haughey government of the Irish Republic the defence minister was one Paddy Power.

GRANNY-POWER ASSERTS ITSELF!

MORE PENSIONER POWER WANTED!!

The rise of rabbi-power

Toddler power's 'save our school' bid

PRACTISING JEW The Jewish equivalent of a 'committed Christian' (see also LAPSED CATHOLIC←). 'Practising homosexuals' are also given this kind of M&S← treatment, though one never reads of practising heterosexuals: perhaps they do not need to practise.

PRETTY A general adjective of admiration, and also a word suggesting a considerable, but not excessive, amount or quantity of anything. The word has changed meanings several times during the last 1000 years or so, beginning with 'craftiness, cunning, artful, astute' and now (in the first of the two senses outlined above) a kind of beauty 'without majesty or stateliness', as the OED prettily puts it. It is interesting to note that when the Princess of Wales was Lady Diana Spencer she was merely pretty, but since her marriage the press has preferred the more majestic and stately adjective. A comma between 'pretty' and the word which follows it may in some instances avoid confusion.

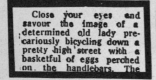

Close your eyes and savour the image of a determined old lady precariously bicycling down a pretty high street with a basketful of eggs perched on the handlebars. The

Margaret is a pretty witty lady of around 45, with a mischievous twinkle an'

The same confusion may apply to the moderate intensification word 'jolly': 'She was a jolly fat lady.'

PROBLEM Both a euphemism and an understatement. When the Apollo 13 space mission encountered what seemed to be calamitous difficulties, including oxygen failure while on the other side of the moon, the calm voice of an astronaut was heard to say, 'We have a problem.' People who are fat admit to having 'a weight problem', drunkards 'an alcohol problem' and couples who quarrel have 'a marital problem'.

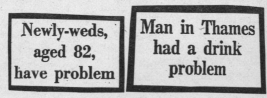

Newly-weds, aged 82, have problem

Man in Thames had a drink problem

THE PROVERBIAL Two words employed to introduce and apologise for an old cliché, as in 'the needle in the proverbial haystack'. See also TO COIN A PHRASE←.

> THE SEARCH for survivors of the Alderney concentration camps so many years after their evacuation was like looking for the needle in the proverbial hay-stack. Many government depart-

PUNDITS, GURUS, MANDARINS, DONS AND WISE MEN 'Pundit' is the anglicised spelling of *pandit*, itself coming from the Sanskrit adjective *pandita*, learned, or skilled. In India *pandit* used to be – and perhaps still is – a kind of courtesy title, much as one might call someone 'professor' even if he does not hold a university chair (or address a tramp as 'squire' or 'colonel'). An Englishman described as a pundit is now more likely to be some expert of the kind interviewed on radio or television (and there are many of them). 'Guru' is the Hindustani word for a teacher or mentor, and only by extension a priest, rather like the Hebrew *rabbi*. Its facetious application to westerners is a comparatively recent fad. Such pundits or gurus are not to be confused with 'wise men', which is the press name for members of a royal commission or other such public body. They, in turn, are different from 'mandarins', originally Chinese officials ('that serue in euery Towne, and haue the gouernment of the same . . . called . . . Mandorijns', as an English traveller wrote in 1598). They are now more likely to be British civil servants, and are usually given an adjectival addition, e.g. 'Whitehall mandarins'. 'Don', for a lecturer or professor at an English university, is Spanish for 'sir', and was first used facetiously by Shakespeare. Female university teachers (or perhaps those who insist on 'Ms' for their address) may soon demand the logical modification to 'donna'.

PURRFECT! Knee-jerk headline or story pun for any story involving – oh, but how clever of you to guess . . .

QUIT News jargon and headline word for 'resign'. People are said in newspapers to 'quit over' a matter, which is not how ordinary people speak or write about a resignation: 'Cancer expert quits over mounting union militancy.' See also OVER←.

RAP 'To strike smartly without causing serious hurt' (*OED*). But a 'rap over the knuckles' is more likely to be figurative, perhaps some kind of public reprimand not intended to cause lasting damage to the victim's career or reputation: altogether a milder form of chastisement than those described under HITTING, SLAMMING AND LASHING OUT←.

RED FACES In newspaper offices all embarrassment is thought to be accompanied by an attack of blushing.

RED LIGHT AREAS Where journalists insist prostitutes ply their trade. When did you last see a red light outside an English brothel? But see GETTING THE GREEN LIGHT←.

ROBIN HOOD Any person who steals but claims to give the proceeds of his theft to the poor, like the mythical medieval English folk-hero.

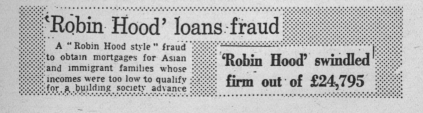

ROLLING In the sense of 'continuing, gradually but relentlessly', this vogue-word has joined 'ongoing'; as in 'rolling devolution' and 'rolling industrial action'.

ROLLING HEADS Essential ingredient of most news stories about sackings or resignations following some scandal or exposure of inefficiency thought to warrant decapitation: 'Heads are expected to roll . . .'

ROMEO Any amorous male, but usually one discomfited by the rejection of his advances to women. From Shakespeare's *Romeo and Juliet*: an inappropriate choice, as the original Romeo's actions were welcomed by his Juliet with open arms.

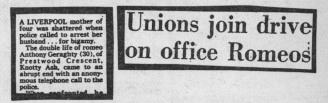

A LIVERPOOL mother of four was shattered when police called to arrest her husband . . . for bigamy.
The double life of romeo Anthony Geraghty (30), of Prestwood Crescent, Knotty Ash, came to an abrupt end with an anonymous telephone call to the police.

Unions join drive on office Romeos

ROTTEN EGGS The chance of finding a rotten egg among fresh or sound ones is about one in several hundred, as every cook will testify. Even then, there is usually no outward sign of rottenness, so that cautious cooks break their eggs first into a cup before adding them, to the food they are preparing. Nevertheless, whenever eggs are thrown by way of public protest they are described in the press as 'rotten'. In other words, 'rotten eggs' is merely an M&S TERM←, devoid of meaning.

and in view of what he has done for the area, it is particularly unfortunate that Mr Heseltine was pelted with rotten eggs when he attempted to open the neigh-

RUMPUS A row, disturbance or uproar; and a favourite headline word. The *OED* says 'probably a fanciful formation', but seems to forget that the Latin word *rumpus* means a vine tendril; so there could be some lost classical allusion to a drunken row. The earliest source quoted is dated 1764: 'Oh, Major! Such a riot and rumpus!' The Americans have added another meaning – 'disorder, mess, untidiness' – and thus gave us the 'rumpus room', where a man can be as untidy as he likes without incurring the disapproval of his wife.

Labour row over expulsion rumpus

College cash rumpus girl rejects place

PAISLEY RUMPUS

CAMPUS HEAD RESIGNATION RUMPUS

Spy Scandal Rumpus

COUNCIL SPENDING RUMPUS

RABBITS RUMPUS

RUN A 'run' on any commodity indicates a special, and possibly artificially stimulated, demand for it.

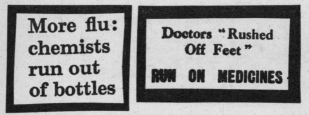

More flu: chemists run out of bottles

Doctors " Rushed Off Feet " RUN ON MEDICINES

SAGA Any story mentioned more than once in the papers qualifies for the title of 'saga'. The word gained new popularity with the showing on BBC television of an adaptation of Galsworthy's *Forsyte Saga*, and a further boost when there were exhibitions and more television programmes about the Vikings in the late 1970s. The *OED* says a saga is any narrative composition in prose written in Iceland and Norway during the Middle Ages but adds, 'In incorrect use (partly as the equivalent of the German *Sage*): a story, popularly believed to be matter of fact, which has been developed by gradual accretions.' Anyone who has read press reports about himself or his family will agree with this definition. Newspaper 'sagas' are usually fitted with a matching M&S← qualification such as 'ongoing', 'continuing', etc. See also DRAMA←.

> THE latest chapter in the on-going saga of Ronald Biggs, 51, Great British-Train Robber at Large, was drawing to a close in Barbados last night.

SAMARITAN A helper, someone who gives aid in a mishap or takes a cup of tea to a neighbour, possibly after a 'mercy' DASH←.

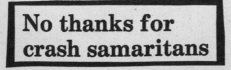

No thanks for crash samaritans

SAUCY Tabloid word for anything titillating or sexually suggestive. It is seldom seen outside newspapers and, when spoken in everyday conversation, is always used in its old sense of impudence or cheek ('Don't give me any sauce!'). The sexual overtones probably came from the popularity of comedians like George Formby and Max Miller, who were both cheeky and smutty.

France's sauciest bed tied up in red tape

The Vicar and those Saucy Pictures

SCENARIO In the theatre, ballet or opera, the outline of the story, plot or action. In news jargon, a circumstance or sequence of events.

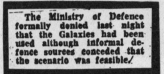

The Ministry of Defence formally denied last night that the Galaxies had been used although informal defence sources conceded that the scenario was feasible.

SCRATCH In sport, to cancel an event or a participation, presumably from scratching out a name from a team list.

British girl has to scratch

SET Expected to happen. The word was first used in headlines, then made its way into text. Apart from the occasional BBC news bulletin written by a fugitive from Fleet Street, 'set' is never heard in ordinary everyday speech. 'Poised' is used in much the same way, and equally stilted, except perhaps in reviews of ballet performances.

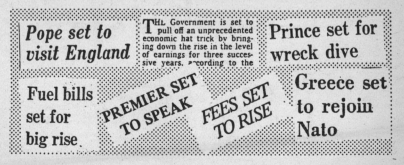

Pope set to visit England

THE Government is set to pull off an unprecedented economic hat trick by bringing down the rise in the level of earnings for three successive years, according to the

Prince set for wreck dive

Fuel bills set for big rise

PREMIER SET TO SPEAK

FEES SET TO RISE

Greece set to rejoin Nato

SHAPELY Tabloid euphemism for a woman with big breasts.

SHELLING OUT Paying for eggs. See below.

SHELL SHOCK A distressing condition which afflicted soldiers during the First World War (and presumably also in the Second, when it would have been given some more scientific or euphemistic name). Today, according to newspapers, shell shock is suffered by housewives when egg prices rise. It is also used as a modification of simple 'shock', without adding anything to it except a superfluous five-letter word.

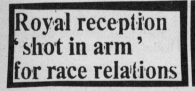

A shell-shocked stock market recovered rapidly yesterday with a rise in the Fina' share. Times ordinary

...ese lamps take standard light bulbs.
Delivery within 28 days. If you're not shell-shocked with delight, return your lamps for a full refund within 30 days.

Shell shock

On Tuesday, Katie Stewart goes to work on an egg: Five days devoted to omelettes, ls, souf.

Those who were not shell-shocked by Blackpool shell-coarsened by it — as were would be after seeing the inside of, say, a borstal

...our years ago, which was the germ of the present plays. He is pleased, if shell-shocked, with the turn around and the publicity of the plays: "It's a bit like

A SHOT IN THE ARM Indiscriminate shooting indulged in by journalists and businessmen. Such shots may be given to the 'lame ducks' of industry. The expression was originally a euphemism for having an alcoholic drink, taken in one gulp, related to 'a shot in the neck' – both Americanisms dating from about 1850. Hence the figurative injection of morale or capital.

Royal reception 'shot in arm' for race relations

yards out. He took five steps and rocketed a shot which Stepney must have seen only as a blur.
It was a shot-in-the-arm which Everton had needed, and roared on by a sud-

SLAPPING ON A price increase.

BP and Esso last night followed Shell's lead and slapped another 5p a gallon on pump prices.

SLAY Archaism surviving only in newspapers. People used to slay each other in Shakespeare (thirty slayings) and the Bible (about four hundred), but who now says, 'Heard this fantastic joke. Listen to this. It'll slay you'?

> The jury will decide whether he was sane or mentally unbalanced when he slew 13 women, and Sir

> And he told the three men whose bungled 'kidnap plot' led to the shotgun slayings: "You will stay in prison until you are very old indeed."

SLICE OF THE CAKE A part of the share. Probably derived from the common statistical diagram showing proportionate figures by means of segments of a circle. So stupefying is the power of clichés that people can in all seriousness compose statements like 'this settlement has to come out of the overall cake available within the social guidelines'.

> *Cities may get bigger slice of the grant cake*

> If a national oil corporation, or even a larger slice of the cake for the nationalised industries, is too much for the Government, then the argument for a form of barrelage tax, on top of royalties,

SMILED, SIGHED, QUIPPED, GRUFFED, etc. Stock openers for old-fashioned journalistic inversions which generally herald BOGUS VERBATIM←. Some say they save time and space by indicating in the shortest possible manner the mood in which the person quoted is said to have said what he is alleged to have said. But it is such a worn-out trick and so far removed from everyday English that it merely sounds silly and stilted.

> CHUCKLED 35 year old trombonist Jim as I interviewed him for the article, 'You were lucky to find me here as an

> A fire officer smiled: "He did mange to get away with a lorry drive'rs most valuable possessions —his log book and his sandwic····." "It's not an artist's job to offer solutions," be gruffed. "I'm not putting forward a programme for the

> QUIPPED Malcolm (24), 'It's just not on, mate. As far as I'm concerned they can stuff it.'

> Sighed shapely divorcee mother of six, Rita (36), "Money is rather short now and I'll have to try and get a job."

SMOKES Newspaper word for 'cigarettes', both in headlines and text. 'Smokes' often go with a PINTA← or CUPPA←. See also MUNCHING←.

SMOKES SET TO RISE

WOMEN: NEW RISKS IN SMOKES

£50,000 smokes stolen

SOAR In nature, birds soar gracefully through the air. But in newspapers the word is prosaically and almost exclusively linked to prices and the cost of living. Things that 'soar' may also PLUNGE AND PLUMMET←.

SPASTIC From the Greek *spasmos*, draw or wrench: an involuntary contraction of the muscles, the noun applied to the unfortunate sufferers from that condition. Sometimes used, with extreme insensitivity, to mean 'clumsy' or 'ungainly' – a usage surely to be deplored, like misapplications of CANCER←, CRUCIFY←, etc.

> but unfortunately when it comes to being a home handywoman, I am absolutely spastic.

SPEAKING OUT To express an opinion with some force.

SPEND, SPEND, SPEND From the personal motto and philosophy of, and title of a book by, a woman who won a fortune on the football pools and lost it again, together with her happiness – and then gained another fortune by describing her experiences. This usage, together with inflation, has helped to drive out the 'spending a penny' euphemism (an old penny was the admission charge to a public lavatory), just as that euphemism drove out the earlier Victorian one in which 'spending' meant orgasm.

The spend-spend holiday Britons

BRITONS spent £7,700 million on their holidays last year.
Those who stayed in Britain spent a record tourism, said the British

joys' for the tourist industry.
● Tourism will play a key role in helping to strengthen Britain's

SPLASH News word meaning big expenditure, or 'splashing out'.

£750,000 SPLASHED BY COUNCIL ON NEW BATHS

SPOTTED MAN A form of acne which appears to afflict wanted men who are recognised in a public place.

Spotted man wanted for questioning

SPOTTED MAN IN STREET

SPOTTED MEN STEALING SALMON
A dock labourer and another man were seen

SPY IN THE CAB The 'tachograph' is a safety device fitted to lorries for measuring and recording speeds, distances and times, etc. and comes from a combination of the Greek words for speed and writing, respectively: indeed 'tachygraphy' was the seventeenth-century word for shorthand, and both 'tachygraph' and 'tachograph' were used until well into the twentieth century for shorthand writers (or stenographers, from *stenos*, close, compressed). Trade union leaders who objected to the introduction of the device in Britain described it as 'a spy in the cab' that would inhibit the freedom of lorry drivers and owners to falsify their records. Newspaper writers always like good, emotive **Names and Nicknames** (page 17), and so the 'spy in the cab' entered the language, just as the aircraft flight recorder became the BLACK BOX←.

SQUEEZE The financial or political 'squeeze' was coined by the Admiralty Secretary Sir Eric Geddes, who said on 9 December 1918: 'We will get everything out of her that you can get out of a lemon and a bit more . . . I will squeeze her until you can hear the pips squeak.' He was referring to Germany, not Lady Geddes.

Minister's squeeze on council spending

STANDS, STANDING FIRM Custer's last stand was only the start of it. In news language 'stands' are generally given extra emphasis with the M&S← addition of 'firm'.

EEC TO STAND FIRM ON OIL

MINISTER TO STAND FIRM ON FISH

BL AND FORD STAND FIRM AGAINST UNIONS

GOVERNMENT STAND FIRM ON WAGES

Joseph stands firm on steel

Councillors Stand Firm on By-pass

Stand on fish zone dropped

PRESIDENT STANDS FIRM ON PIPELINE

STATE GRAB Headline abbreviation for 'nationalisation'. The recently coined reverse process is 'privatisation'. When nationalised industries in the 'public sector' are offered for sale they are always said in the press to be UP FOR GRABS←. 'Grabbing' has long been a word dear to the news media. In 1873 'salary grab' was on many American lips and in the contemporary press, defined later as an opprobrious term for the Act of the United States Congress of 1873 by which congressmen acquired the power to increase their own salaries, as MPs have in Britain.

STRATEGIC PLACES In the papers, always sexual; but in ancient Greece a *strategos* was a commander-in-chief or a chief magistrate. Strategy is the art of planning larger military operations, the immediate or local ones being tactics. Thus the nuclear bomb is a strategic weapon, the field gun a tactical one. But in the press, strategy has nothing to do with warfare, at any rate of the conventional kind. If the Book of Genesis had been written in Fleet Street, chapter 3, verse 7 would have read: 'and they sewed fig leaves together, and made themselves aprons, strategically placed'. The media men have got it all wrong, of course. 'Come up and see my etchings' is *strategy*; but a groping hand travelling upwards from a lady's knee towards 'strategic places' would be *tactics*.

STRING OF RACE-HORSES Although this is not the recognised collective noun for horses, race-horses when mentioned in the press as being under someone's ownership always come in 'strings'; never a 'string of cart-horses' or a 'string of ponies'.

STRUCTURE A word frequently and quite needlessly tacked on to other words, adding nothing except verbiage: 'wages structure', 'careers structure', etc. Many things may now be 'structured' – from suits to brassières and jobs.

SUNK, SCUPPERED, TORPEDOED AND CAPSIZED When maritime or other watery projects run into difficulties, they are invariably described in one of half a dozen obligatory maritime terms: they 'sail into stormy (or troubled) waters', 'capsize', are 'torpedoed', 'scuppered', or merely 'sunk'. But when things are going well, it may be a case of 'full steam ahead' (that some fifty years after steam began to disappear from the oceans); even more absurdly, they may be 'sailing high' – an amphibious form of locomotion possible only in newspaper offices, and based, of course, on the FLYING HIGH← cliché.

The torpedo, incidentally, was a fish long before it became a weapon of war, which was named with unusual imagination and aptness. The Latin word *torpedo* means stiffness or numbness (compare 'torpor'); and the fish, which has an almost circular body with a tapering tail, just like the more deadly metal fish, has the capacity for emitting electrical shocks that numb those who get in its way. The explosive torpedo was devised at the beginning of the nineteenth century, during the Napoleonic Wars.

SUPER- George Bernard Shaw began it in a small way with his play *Man and Superman* (1903), but 'super-' as a media cliché prefix did not become really popular until the *Superman* films and television programmes of the 1950s. The fashion was given impetus by a 'Vicky' cartoon in the London *Evening Standard* (6 November 1958), showing the prime minister, Mr Harold Macmillan, dressed as Superman and labelled 'Supermac'. Ever since, the prefix has been applied to anything slightly larger or better than normal: 'super-rats', 'super-bees', 'super-mice'. Police informers, 'grasses' in underworld slang, become 'super-grasses' (hyphenation is optional) when they inform on bigger criminals; substitute players in soccer who often score, 'supersubs'; excessively fertile parents 'supermums' or 'superdads'; and young tennis stars (or 'superstars' – a popular showbusiness description applied even to Jesus Christ) 'superbrats' when they throw tantrums.

TALKS Can be the third person singular or a plural noun, and therefore a source of confusion.

TEETHING TROUBLES Early and supposedly unavoidable difficulties with a new project; from the pain experienced by infants when teething. Unfortunately the expression has lost all its force; as witness the fact that teething troubles are usually said to be 'ironed out'.

TIGHT LIPPED (AND ASHENFACED) Newsworthy people who have just suffered some kind of humiliation, such as being sacked from an important job, e.g. a football manager or prime minister, seldom wish to talk to reporters. 'He hurried away, tight lipped and ashenfaced' is the standard parrot phrase in such reports.

> **BIRKENHEAD Councillor Roy Perkins was staying tightlipped yesterday about the circumstances which prompted him to**
>
> Mears said: "I want to be as tight lipped as possible about this. All I can say is that Geoff has left the club."
>
> Government officials were last night tight-lipped about the reasons for Mr Turton's decision. .'

TIRED AND EMOTIONAL Drunk. The purpose of the euphemism is to avoid possible lawsuits for defamation, as drunkenness is a temporary condition and very difficult to prove in retrospect. Aneurin Bevan won a huge sum in damages against a journalist and his paper for describing him as drunk, which is exactly what he was (as postumously confirmed in Richard Crossman's diaries). Had the journalist said he was 'tired and emotional as a newt' he would probably have got away with it.

TO COIN A PHRASE What the writer means is usually to apologise for yet again flogging an old cliché. See THE PROVERBIAL←.

TONGUE LASHING The fiercest possible verbal attack imaginable by a newsman. On radio 'getting the rough edge of his tongue' has been heard in the same context.

See also HITTING, SLAMMING AND LASHING OUT←.

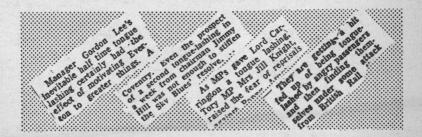

TRACK RECORDS AND LEAGUE TABLES News items are often presented in sporting terms.

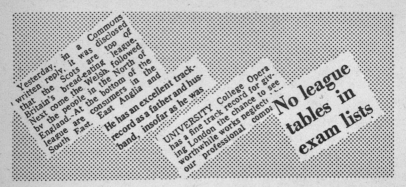

Yesterday, in a Commons written reply, it was disclosed that the Scots are top of Britain's bread-eating league. Next come the Welsh, followed by the people in the North of England. At the bottom of the league are consumers in the South East. East Anglia and

He has an excellent track-record as a father and hus-band, insofar as he was

UNIVERSITY College Opera has a fine track record for giv-ing London the chance to see worthwhile works neglect our professional comp

No league tables in exam lists

TRAUMA The Greek word for 'wound', meaningfully employed in the appropriate context by doctors, who know what they are talking about. The rest of us use it more loosely, and nearly always inaccurately, as in the cutting shown here. An 'insidious trauma that refuses to die' is an interesting but unlikely idea.

> The Motherwell episode sticks in my mind the clearest — like an insidious trauma that refuses to die. It all started at Stirling Station where I jumped on a train thinking it

TRIO The Italian word for a set of three has been commandeered by headline-writers for its brevity and soon took its place in text and even in formal BBC news bulletins. It gives the news an incongruously musical flavour. Media 'trios' can be singular or plural. See also THE 'FAMOUS FIVE' CLICHÉ←.

CONMEN TRIO ARRESTED

DRUG TRIO HANGED
Three drug traffickers were hanged in Malaysia yesterday. Malaysian courts are getting

New Trio goes to Lords

Tory trio hope

Trio on kidnap charge

TURBULENCE What aerial or maritime projects run into when things are not going smoothly or FLYING HIGH←.

> TURBULENCE and dissension are swirling round an ambitious scheme to raise the Tudor warship Mary Rose from her grave in the mud 50 ft beneath the Solent.

'(TO) UP' To increase. There is a nautical basis for the usage, for sailors have long spoken of 'upping' anchors, sails, etc. The word looks better in headlines than in body matter of news stories, and sounds bad in spoken English – but at least it is short and unpretentious, which is more than can be said for 'jacking up' or, worse, 'ameliorating the wages and salaries infrastructure'. There is always the threat that, unless wages are 'upped', tools may be 'downed'.

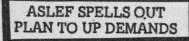

ASLEF SPELLS OUT
PLAN TO UP DEMANDS

Pretoria ups its
arms spending

UP FOR GRABS Journalists' slang for 'available', 'for sale'. See STATE GRAB←.

UPFRONT American jargon of the 1970s. Wentworth and Flexner give it in the supplement, meaning 'in advance' ('But I never asked for cash "up front" because that strikes me as too whorish' – Xaviera Hollander, *The Happy Hooker*) and also 'honest, truthful, out in the open' ('she's intelligent, politically aware, and very up-front about who she is and what she thinks' – James Nolan, *The Third Sex*). As so often happens with new American jargon, trendy journalists (especially, it must be said, those who fill the women's pages) adopt such terms eagerly and flog them to death, perhaps because it makes them feel a little more up-front than their readers.

> There is something to be said for Dr Charny's argument. Two couples whom I know very well and who seem to be still as interested in each other as they ever were are notoriously up-front about their hostility. Their sparring matches are the despair of hostesses, and house guests have

VOW 'I vow to thee, my country . . .' we sing at school, and later perhaps make solemn marriage vows. But apart from that, vows never enter our daily vocabulary. The papers, however, after first pressing vows into service for headlines, have debased them into a synonym for any decision, however mundane or trivial.

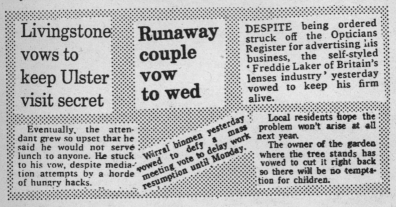

Livingstone vows to keep Ulster visit secret

Runaway couple vow to wed

DESPITE being ordered struck off the Opticians Register for advertising his business, the self-styled ' Freddie Laker of Britain's lenses industry' yesterday vowed to keep his firm alive.

Eventually, the attendant grew so upset that he said he would not serve lunch to anyone. He stuck to his vow, despite mediation attempts by a horde of hungry hacks.

Wirral binmen yesterday vowed to defy a mass meeting vote to delay work resumption until Monday.

Local residents hope the problem won't arise at all next year.

The owner of the garden where the tree stands has vowed to cut it right back so there will be no temptation for children.

WALKABOUT Ordinary people walk, dogs 'go walkies', but royalty, prime ministers and other important persons 'go walkabout'. The primitive-sounding formation betrays its origin – the Australian outback, where it is the aboriginals' term for a walk through the country or bush, or idle and aimless wandering. It has long been part of Australian speech but entered newspaper language during a British royal visit to Australia in the 1950s.

WALKING AWAY AND WALKING FREE People accused of an offence but acquitted at their trial are always described as having 'walked free' from court, with sometimes an implied suggestion that they were lucky to have got away with it. In fact they may not even 'walk' but be WHISKED AWAY← by the 'representative' of a newspaper practising chequebook journalism. Those who survive an accident are similarly said to have 'walked away' ('without a scratch'), even if they were severely shocked and in no fit state to walk.

Ritchie walks free

A 31-year-old mother of two who killed her husband with a chopper because he wanted to whip her walked free from a court yesterday.

A JEALOUS husband who tried to win back the love of his estranged wife in a shotgun and bill hook battle walked free from a court yesterday.

A 23-YEAR-OLD Liverpool man walked free from court yesterday after he was cleared on seven charges arising out of last

A TEENAGER who killed her stepfather when he tried to rape her walked free from a court yesterday.

Joyriders Walk Away After Crash: Two Held

WATCHDOGS Persons who watch over our interests. When there are several of them working together, they become 'watchdog bodies'. Not to be confused with 'dogsbodies', or even dogs' bodies.

Labour scheme for top watchdog to vet advertising

Government 'should set up health watchdog'

Britain is being condemned to a much smaller railway system because of govern- ment policy towards British Rail, the rail consumer watch- dog body said yesterday.

More roadside toilets needed, say watchdogs

WEATHER CONDITIONS The second word is unnecessary, as in 'Because of the worst weather conditions for a century . . .' 'Situation' is similarly misused, but extensive ridicule by satirists has almost put an end to its reign, except among sports commentators.

WED Fleet Street archaism. No one talks like that except in Mummerzet and newspapers: 'Darling, when I'm a sub-editor shall we be wed?'

Islamabad (AP) – An unwed mother who killed her newborn baby has been sentenced to die by hanging by a district court in Dera Ismail Khan, newspapers

'YOU CAN'T JAIL ME—I'M TO BE WED'

WEEPING OPENLY (or UNASHAMEDLY) An M&S TERM←. Newsmen know no other way of publicly showing grief.

General Mario Menendez, the defeated Argentine mili- tary governor of the Falk- lands, wept openly after he surrendered his forces at Port Stanley and was refused permission to join his demo-

WHIRLWIND ROMANCE A newspaper term seldom or never heard in real conversation by real people.

WHISKED AWAY This is what happens to royalty or politicians after 'going' WALKABOUT← or to people in whom the press shows some special, and usually disreputable, interest: perhaps defendants or litigants in a law-suit who are thought to have a story worth buying. So they are 'whisked away' before they inadvertently give a quotable statement to rival journalists. See WALKING AWAY←

> They left the court hand in hand to be whisked away by taxi, accompanied by representatives of a Sunday newspaper.
> Docherty, 53, the former Manchester United and Scot

WHITEWASH Excuses or justifications, or attempts to make things appear better than they are.

> as spokesman for the black community of Brixton, I can only describe the Scarman Report as whitewash.

> He told a London Industrial Tribunal : " I was blackmailed into covering up discrepancies in the accounting. Because I was Indian, everything I complained of was whitewashed. They just whitewashed any complaint — thinking I am a helpless man and I can't do anything.'

WHOLESALE On a large scale. Wholesalers sell goods to retailers.

> "I have no doubt that there is now every possibility of wholesale bankruptcy in petrol retailing," he said.
> Cheap sensationalism about the

WILDERNESS This appears to have been something of a vogue word among early translators of the Bible. Whether it was Hebrew *yeshimon*, *midbar*, *arabah*, *tsiyyah*, *tohu*, or Greek *eremos*, *eremia* – each specifying some particular kind of inhospitable, desolate or waterless place – the translators always appear to have plumped for 'wilderness'. Today's translators probably prefer their biblical characters to cry from an 'ecologically disadvantaged environment'. Journalistic wildernesses are always metaphorical and frequently political; when those banished to a 'political wilderness' return to favour, they are said to **Come in from the cold** (see page 24).

THE CAMPAIGN for the Revitalisation of Ale claimed yesterday that the North of England would become a "beer drinker's wilderness" unless urgent action was

AFTER seven years in the wilderness, he came in from the cold on election to the commons after the death of the sitting member.

WINDING UP To anyone who grew up with clockwork toys, winding something up means making it go – giving it power. The *OED* devotes more than two dozen columns to 'wind' in all its forms, both pronunciations and hundreds of meanings. I guess that winding up a firm has more than a figurative connection with the winding-sheet used to wrap up a corpse; and from 'winding up' we doubtless get the slang expression 'that about wraps it up' (in broadcasting or television, both 'winding' and 'wrapping' up refers to the closing remarks).

Clegg to be wound up at end of the year

MECCANO TO BE WOUND UP

WRAPS Things are 'kept under wraps' when secrecy is observed; the 'wraps are off' when revelations are made, or plans 'unveiled'. An archaism which dates back to the sixteenth century and is seldom seen or heard outside newspapers.

TODAY the wraps come off Vauxhall's new World car with the official unveiling of the all-new Cavalier.

Yesterday county council chairman Councillor Neville Goldrein took the wraps off a special plan which is designed to split caused

HEFTY increases in drink, cigarettes, petrol and VAT were unveiled in a tough budget in Ireland yesterday.

YEN A unit of Japanese currency, and headline cliché for stories about Orientals and their likings, cravings or yearnings: as in 'having a yen for', which is an American abbreviation (c 1930) of the Chinese word yen-shee, opium. The Japanese coin comes from the Chinese word yüan, round, round thing, so journalists who use 'yen' headlines indiscriminately for all Far Eastern stories are not so far wrong.

YEN FOR 'DECADENT'

THE Communist authorities trying to stop people in Southern China from tuning in to "decadent" Hongkong television stations, but most

Yen to learn

A Japanese college for women is to be opened at Winchester later this month. Shoei College in Tokyo, will annually send 20 students to Winchester Shoei College to learn English and absorb the culture of Britain.

Pit Your Skill against the Press

A News Quiz of Confusions, Solecisms and Malapropisms*

Any number of people can play this game, taking entries by turns and agreeing on the number of marks they should award each other. Or play it on your own, giving yourself one mark for spotting an error and two for re-phrasing each extract as it should have been written. A blank space is provided for this purpose to the right of each cutting. Maximum number of marks=384. If you score 350 or more, especially without recourse to the Oxford English Dictionary, you should have written this book. Score 50 marks or fewer – and you may apply for a job at your nearest newspaper. For answers and suggestions for re-phrasing please see pages 160 onwards.

*Mrs Malaprop: a character in Sheridan's play The Rivals (1775), who was in the habit of confusing words that sounded alike.

Pit Your Skill against the Press

Write your corrections here, possibly re-phrasing as you consider appropriate.

"It was only a 50-50 chance that I would ever walk again and I also developed agrophobia.

1

"They (the Jews) see the Cuban refugees as an allegory of the Soviet Jews." They have donated more than 7½ tons of clothing and

2

he said that the prisoner had two arms and a leg decapitated, so as to prevent him from escaping.

3

when the Family Planning Association (FPA) opened an anti-natal clinic. It never expected the success and popularity it met with. And

4

Paul said, 'We're just good friends', but when pressed admitted he and Linda were anticipating marriage.

5

KIM HUGHES (above) was appointed yesterday as Australia's captain for the series of one-day internationals which starts tomorrow.

6

is said to rank among Mrs
Thatcher's most aciduous
supporters - one who can
always be relied on to act

7

It is widely predicted that the
forthcoming space flight by
the American cosmonauts will
be the most successful ever. It

8

then there is also the point
that the Ford workers get
wages that are astronomic-
ally lower than Leylands.

9

Park benches have been
repainted, and the grass
is being cut - all to give
notice that the weather
is getting barmier every
day. Temperatures of
over 60 deg. have been
recorded already.

*It is surely one of the
Health Authority's
balmier suggestions
that doctors should be
obliged to sign such*

10

The changeover of power in
Washington became almost a
sideshow as the country waited
with baited breath to hear if
the aircraft carrying the 52
Americans had taken off from
Tehran.

11

Canonization takes time, of course ;
unless the Pope himself makes a
special dispensation, beautification
can only take place 50 years after a
candidate's death.

12

The borough of Rochdale is
trying to trace about a dozen
paintings, part of a collection
bequested by a local indus-
trialist, Thomas Kay, which
may be worth £1 million.

13

when charged, the accused
blenched visibly, so that his
face turned as white as a
sheet. But in every other
way he kept his composure,

14

Detectives hunting the killer
of Mrs Susan Vorswick, a 28-
year-old blond divorcee, want
to interview a man who took
her home after a night out.

15

journey gives me a few hours
without interruptions of any
sort. To have no telephone
calls is the greatest boom.
Nothing is more frustrating
than to have a promising line

16

and at Pilkingtons and its associated
works, a bottleneck has caused another delay in glass production. b-

IT IS ESTIMATED that the strike
will cause the biggest ever bottleneck in radiator production since

17

It centres around Kelmscott House, the charming three-storey building on the banks of the Thames at Hammersmith, where Morris lived from 1878 to 1896. He

This fictional investigation centres around a TV studio interview in which two hard-nosed sceptics quiz a Mrs Bridget Hitler (Siobhan McKenna) about the validity of her memoirs.

18

Carmania stuck fast on unchartered coral island

19

it is the immigrant shopkeepers who have persuaded the local merchants that the way to increase turnover is to lengthen their hours and cheapen their wares. Only in this way is

20

when suddenly my car left the road and after swerving from side to side, collided with a tree. Fortunately I was wearing my seat belt and

21

Next week at the London Colosseum the English National Opera will be giving Smetana's Bartered Bride, with a cast that is

22

She is Petty Officer Linda Murray, aged 17, of 49 Castleway North, Leasowe, and she will sail from Portsmouth on May 28 and be at sea until June 10. She will be a member of the crew compromising girls from all over the country.

23

There is said to be yet another tunnel scheme in the pipeline, but at present it is considered far too costive to have any possible chance of acceptance.

24

Call for ban on 'cowboy drivers'

25

porter; when he reproved Mr Xavier he was told: "Listen mate, if you want to take on me and the portering staff you would be faced with strikes and noncooperation".

With coworkers Friederich W Busch and Eddie T Wei,

have not passed by at all: the British, to Moritz's amused irritation, are frequently coy about such matters and simply omit the name of their coproducer.

For many years he was a cowriter on the Archers programme of the BBC.

According to Mr Joseph Andrews, the cochairman of the committee, its aim is to " bring about consciousness-raising with

26

The very thought of this man behaving like that stretches my credibility to breaking-point.

and with it the President has lost any credulity he ever had with the moder-

27

FOUR THOUSAND people are calling for a public inquiry into a planned expressway which will cut a swathe through one of the most populated areas of Warrington.

28

QUANGOS
TO BE
DECIMATED

29

ITALIANS
IN CUP
DELIRIUM

30

The Luanda trial was not concerned with justice, but with propaganda. Some of the men may have received their true desserts; others may spend years in gaol simply because of a

31

mand. The order to desist from his campaign came directly, he was told, from 10 Downing Street.

32

about. I stood beside the Lord Mayor and Lady Mayoress during the first half which lasted two hours and it was very tiring and very hot. At the interval, we went downstairs for a coffee, and because of the discomfiture I suggested to the Lord Mayor that it would be quite alright if he and the Lady Mayoress prefered not to return for

33

the house has barely been altered since the year 1547 during the disillusionment of the monasteries by King Henry VIII, who requisition-

34

when he arrived at court, the judge was told that Hopkins had been driven from his home by his wife.

35

Patterson, the cultural attaché who epitomises Australian refinement in his powder-blue safari suit soaked in beer stains, druling saliva and self-importance over the front row of the stalls. It moves

36

cold germ decimated the Eskimos, laying waste the very heart of simple communities and reducing them to dye-stamps of London and New York, with all the accompanying ills of greed.

37

Mr Thorpe appeared charismatic and dominant. One council member said: 'We felt the only people who would be against the appointment would be died-in-the-wool reactionaries.'

38

He is a big man, with a powerful physique and a strong, clear beat, but the symphony sounded more than a little effete and lacking in rhythm. If

39

As a useful and energetic chief executive for the Isle of Anglesey, the late Peredur Lloyd brought to his job a distinctive style and verve which were refreshing and enervating.

40

Such is the enormity of the project, an adaptation - of Paul Scott's epic The Raj Quartet, that transmission is not expected before the winter of 1983-4.

Preparatory work the

Mr Stockwell gave reams of facts and figures detailing the enormity of the police effort, recounted endless facets of the investigation and categorically denied

41

It ordered all Ugandans living in areas occupied by the invaders to evacuate.

42

for his "treachery." But since they could not get at him in a closely guarded top-security jail, they decided to extract their vengeance on his brother.

43

so it was decided to call upon Father Bernard to come to the pub and exercise the ghost. It

44

COUNCILLOR Sefton said that ratepayers were openly flaunting rate demands and refusing to pay.

Pools winner Mrs Marie Jones declared that her life would be the same as before and her neighbours would not be seeing her flouting her new wealth.

After his abortive five-minute stay in the street, the ice-cream driver slowly eased out the clutch and moved forward. Would he, I thought, dare flaunt the recent recommendations so soon after the Government had shown its mettle?

45

Mr Shaw was a survivor of HMS Thetis, the submarine which floundered off the shore in Liverpool Bay in 1939.

46

through the NHS when as a medical practitioner he is forbidden from advertising them in the normal public manner

47

Mrs Margaret Simey, chairman of Meseyside Police Committee, made this point forcibly last night and said she thought it disgraceful that the police should be asked to deal with young children. That responsibility, ... should be

Sir: Alexander Chancellor's report (21 March) of the vile treatment of a 20-year-old student by a London branch of the Midland Bank forcibly takes me back to the Oxford of 1946, where I was an ex-RAF married undergraduate at Wadham.

48

move within 30 days from a beach house owned by her one-time lesbian lover, the tennis star, Billie-Jean King, a judge ruled yesterday.

49

it was almost a foregone conclusion that young Arthur would join H.M. Prison Service to become a jailer. He has now seen service in some of the most secure gaols in the

50

siderable peril, and noticed some tiles had shifted. So I got onto the roof man and asked him to come round. He didn't turn up, and the first big rain did the rest. He is

51

Later, accused asked Mrs Reddington if she could fill her hot water bottle from the geezer in the kitchen. Afterwards, Mrs Reddington

52

tained no serious interest in politics. But crisis can turn capitalism and revolution into strange bedfellow's.

(Diary, December 8) suggests that contraceptives thrown from the Lord's public gallery during a recent debate on abortion, might have caused offence. However, for some of us the only "offensive" objects to be found on the floor were certain of their lordships.

ᴬᵘˢᵗᵃⁿᵗ.
The memorial, at Irby Branch Library, will take the form of a framed collage of Private Lester Memorabilia prepared by Mr Denis Rose who has a sweet's and tobacconist's shop in nearby Greasby.

advanced factories, I see Manchester is investing it's money on the results of a report that 15 million passengers can be attracted to Manchester airport by the 1990s.

Set back to Bigg's instant freedom

And its saving BL more than a million pounds a year.

make up the race relations community — by now there must be hundred's of thousands of them — also have the right

53

A WALLASEY man yesterday escaped certain death by less than a hare's breath when an electricity pylon he was working on was struck by a fl...

54

Five years ago Howell was in the thick of the hiccup the miners brought about in the power supplies which was exacerbated by the Arab oil embargo. He spent six weeks at

55

And, right in front of the Gwladys Street hoards—the equivalent of Anfield's Kop—Grobbelaar then produced two breath-taking saves to protect Liverpool's lead and maintain their challenge for the First Division title.

market too late. Doesn't she know that they are all sold by 10 am? We ravening hoards up here always buy our pheasants early — before

56

Gossips'
victim
hung
himself

Minutes after watching the blazing building on TV. she went outside and hung herself with her coat belt.

57

sory medical attention. He has lost 50 lb. weight and is suffering from malnutrition, hypotension and a kidney complaint.

He changed his mind, slipped
aboard the vessel and hid for
nine hours in the hold where
the temperature was —23C. He
was found suffering from
severe frostbite in his knees
and feet and acute hyper-
thermia. Doctors at a Vancouver hospital are assessing

58

Bradford and Leicester
are among the cities with
the highest concentration
of Asian emigrants, many
of them now prosperous

59

Sami Shidiak, commander
of the Lebanese forces in the
Christian enclaves separating
Israel from the terrorist-
infected areas further north,
said in Israel yesterday that
unless Jerusalem decided to

and it was at first thought
that he was infested with
the deadly Green Monkey
disease virus which has so
far baffled many doctors.

60

I would also claim a decent pat-
riotism but, against Antony Flew
(October 3), I would not see this as
incompatible with criticism of my
country's institutions. More particularly I believe Professor Gould's
pamphlet to be inimicable to the
essential idea of a university.
Yours faithfully,

61

had suffered a cardiac arrest after the fall, most likely caused through inhaling his own vomit. He suffered irreversible b r a i n damage as a result.

62

come the autumn and the annual spate of party political conferences, and the town sees a great many extra-political goings on and high jinx.

63

came the high spot in his career when he was summoned to Buckingham Palace to be benighted by the Queen.

64

It had the word URGENT written largely across the top of the envelope. From

65

A 43-YEAR-OLD Wirral man took his own life by laying in front of a train, an inquest at Bromborough heard yesterday.

ANY TEAM that marches into Anfield behind a banner proclaiming them the "Team of the 'Eighties" is bound to meet the full fury of a champion's sting. Liverpool, winners throughout the 'seventies, heard the advancing trumpets of the precocious, talented Londoners and laid in wait.

with the lack of concern with the saving of the lives of men within the submarine Thetis, not when it was laying at the bottom of the sea off the Great Orme in 1939, but when

Mrs Williams favoured the leader being elected by one-man one-vote. But Mr Jenkins and Mr Rodgers argued instead the choice should lay with the SDP's MPs and they won the day by 2 to 1 majority.

Uneasy lays the head that wears the crown, as Mr Rupert Murdoch found in his first year as a Fleet Street press lord.

Britons in Iran warned: Lay low

66

The legendary legless fighter pilot, Group Captain Sir Douglas Bader, who is credited with downing at least 22 nazi war-planes, has been

67

Mr Jones gave a somewhat lifeless and limpid performance of the sonata. That

68

Put all the ingredients into a blender with a half cup of stock and liquidate the whole to a creamy consistency. It may

69

Let me say straight away that I would loath being without my freezer now. It is undoubtedly a boon in

was about 98 per cent successful, but people involved in the twilight zones where attacks occurred were often loathe to co-operate.

"Some prostitutes will risk

70

are all short-lived items such as bus tickets, election leaflets, sales circulars, etc., which the trade calls momentoes. Prices

Sixty wedding. momentos, many with pictures of the Prince of Wales. and Lady Diana Spencer, are being sold in the shop. They range from

71

After halftime, Liverpool were more on their metal, and an entertaining game developed.

CADMIUM is a different kind of mettle altogether, hard and resistant to rusting.

72

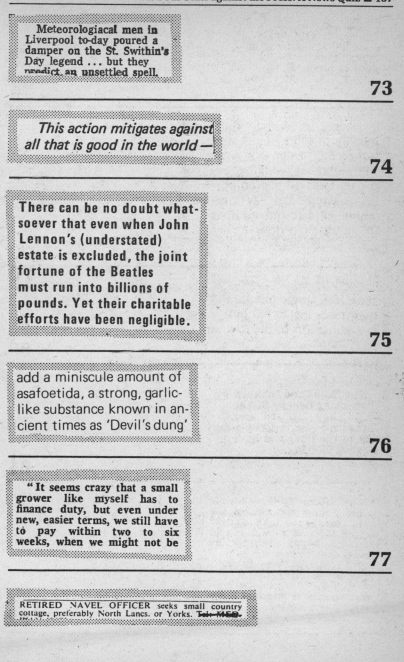

Meteorologiacal men in Liverpool to-day poured a damper on the St. Swithin's Day legend ... but they predict an unsettled spell.

73

This action mitigates against all that is good in the world —

74

There can be no doubt what- soever that even when John Lennon's (understated) estate is excluded, the joint fortune of the Beatles must run into billions of pounds. Yet their charitable efforts have been negligible.

75

add a miniscule amount of asafoetida, a strong, garlic- like substance known in an- cient times as 'Devil's dung'

76

" It seems crazy that a small grower like myself has to finance duty, but even under new, easier terms, we still have to pay within two to six weeks, when we might not be

77

RETIRED NAVEL OFFICER seeks small country cottage, preferably North Lancs. or Yorks. Tel: ~~M50~~.

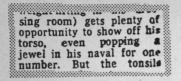

sing room) gets plenty of
opportunity to show off his
torso, even popping a
jewel in his naval for one
number. But the tonsils

78

neighbourhood. They were
not pleased when one night
the sounds of twanging electric guitars and deafening
drums were heard. A noisome
pop group had moved into
the house next door.

79

and every single one had
their faces inspected before admission to the low

80

Her husband chased
them along Granby Street
until they stopped and
turned on him, knocking
him to the floor and then
stealing £500 in notes.

81

The ground was cleared for
Lord Soames to take specific
action, short of a total ban in
a party, by an ordnance he
issued last Wednesday.
This enables him to take
three intermediary stepps:

A restriction of meetings order;

82

Like all good stories it has its surprises—quite apart from the disclosure that, since 1952, it is the Home Secretary who has been responsible for overlooking security.

83

fourteen month old son, who has undergone cleft palette repair, having already had plastic surgery to repair his unilateral cleft lip.

● A pregnant wine writer sounds almost a contradiction in terms, though possibly only to those who do not realize how much we dedicated students of the grape expectorate. I have been extraordinarily lucky in escaping morning sickness, and finding my pallet changed only as far as a short-lived distaste for alcohol in the all important early months,

row. Debbie is writing home to describe the inmates of her flat, a tribe of fellow countrywomen who swarm and totter about the toilet and landings making chocolate cakes and sleeping in numberless confusion on strewn palettes. Debbie is meticulous in naming each girl and wherever possible her

84

Eighteenth-century dilettantes like their bibelots exotic and ingenious; James Cox of Shoe Lane, London, catered to this taste, providing richly-ornamented automaton clocks. one

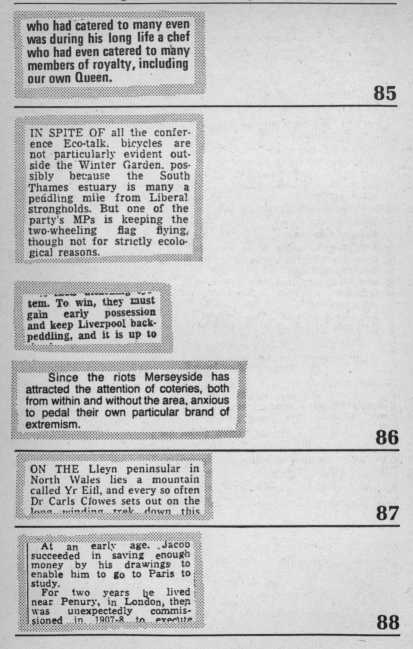

who had catered to many even
was during his long life a chef
who had even catered to many
members of royalty, including
our own Queen.

85

IN SPITE OF all the conference Eco-talk, bicycles are
not particularly evident outside the Winter Garden, possibly because the South
Thames estuary is many a
peddling mile from Liberal
strongholds. But one of the
party's MPs is keeping the
two-wheeling flag flying,
though not for strictly ecolo-
gical reasons.

tem. To win, they must
gain early possession
and keep Liverpool back-
peddling, and it is up to

Since the riots Merseyside has
attracted the attention of coteries, both
from within and without the area, anxious
to pedal their own particular brand of
extremism.

86

ON THE Lleyn peninsular in
North Wales lies a mountain
called Yr Eifl, and every so often
Dr Carls Clowes sets out on the
long winding trek down this

87

At an early age, Jacob
succeeded in saving enough
money by his drawings to
enable him to go to Paris to
study.
For two years he lived
near Penury, in London, then
was unexpectedly commis-
sioned in 1907-8 to execute

88

Applicants will receive bonus increments of up to £100.00 per anum, as considered to be appropriate by the managers.

89

"Every time I play a theatre. I ask for a couple." says Denzar, 67. "I remember the Shakespeare had the most

When veteran New Orleans drummer Freddie Kohlman plays the Bell Hotel, Sadlergate, Derby, tonight, he will bring with him a beat that pre-dates the recorded history of jazz. African drums,

"I was always amazingly lucky. When I started "there were reps in every town, two or three theatres. I began in a bad way, acting in all sorts of places. Do you know, I've actually played *swimming baths,* and the Town Hall, Staines.
"But I'd played Vanya and Parolles in Birmingham Rep by the time I was 24, and I'd also

"It's like playing the Niagara Falls," says Ralph. "Playing the organ is one great ego trip and anyone who tells you anything different is a liar."

90

gatherings. Matty, also at Harvard, pours water and collects dirty dishes until midnight in a local restaurant. You can almost smell the work ethic in the air. Daughter Katy, a pre-Raphaeliate 16-year-old pours over brochures worrying about which college to choose. She

゜ere nave been no replies. But Emma is as determined as ever and is pouring over all the books she can find.

sai y. wnicn could be torn up, and which could be improved.

After months of pouring over the intricacies of the forms selected, the civil servants found that about a quarter could be abandoned.

The pioneering work of the review teams, under the direction of Sir Derek Rayner, the Prime Minister's adviser on

91

With the sense of timing that tennis pros might envy, he is opening his film at a Royal premier on June 18 just as this year's Wimbledon "cast" are flying into town

92

and as we were talking, their Swedish au pair entered and pressed an egg on him. He didn' t seem to object.

93

On the eve of publication of this year's short list for the country's most prestigious and often controversial literary award. I can reveal that the reclusive Australian White's

94

What Mr Whitelaw is putting in its way is rather interesting. The two principle offences which lurkers are watched under "suss" were thieving of or from cars and handbag snatching.

added that there were no two ways about it. It was a matter of principal and that can

95

FATHER Murphy said in his address that it was the duty of all good Catholic parents to see to the procuration of children. Thus, he said, it had ever been.

96

Sentence of 15 years for Abbott

Jack Henry Abbott, literary celebrity and prodigy of the novelist Norman Mailer, was yesterday sentenced to 15 years to life for killing Richard Adan, a part-time waiter, last summer. Disregarding the defence's

97

much as they tried, they
were totally unable to
pry open the door, which
was totally jammed from
the inside. In the end

98

After the riots the council
and businesses organised an
" I'm Backing Brixton ". campaign, with a public relations
rassmatazz of badges, posters
and T-shirts. Those in Bri

pionship, to be held in a
London ballroom with the
usual desperate razzmar-
tazz.

January 22, that to hold a
Yankee-style razzamataz
over events in Poland is
superficial, apart from the
sickening question of the
double standards of lead-
ing politicians. Talk about

THE PUBLICITY which attends the Booker Prize
for Fiction may one day be compared by sociologists
yet unborn with the razmataz which attends other
seemingly minority interests, such as darts or
wrestling. For in a country as comparatively

99

It was only after a protracted law suit that he found himself unable to get recompense for the injuries he suffered in the accident, and

100

Cameras, film and sound

News of the release of Julian Manyon, 31, a reporter, Ted Adock, 39, a cameraman and Trefor Hunter, 38, a sound recorder, was given to Thames by Norman Fenton, their reporter who escaped on foot

by unknown assailants.

Mr Julian Manyon, aged 31, was taken away in a Ford Falcon car and the other two, Mr Edward Adcock, aged 40, the cameraman, and Mr Trefor Hunter, aged 38, the sound recordist, were taken away in another vehicle.

101

" Their whole behaviour wreaked of it. They were extremely professional and throughout it all they were in contact with somebody over a built-in radio in their car. They

'It was sheer mayhem,' he said. 'They were reeking vengeance - that was their only object - and no-one could stop them.'

102

accused said there was nothing
he could reply in the light of
what Mr Hawkins had said -but
he totally refuted the charge.

103

The subject may be repel-
lant, but I think that can
always be excused if the
treatment is correct."
Mr Newman's career has

104

................against him, in
spiracy and distribution charges. Co-defendant
Roshan, (34), a Washington restauranteur, w
on a single

105

WE WISH OUR READERS .
A RESTIVE CHRISTMAS -
AND A PROSPEROUS
NEW YEAR

106

M Ps SIDESTEP
OFFER OF TALKS
IN TEHERAN

An attempt by the Govern-
ment of Iran to attract British
M Ps from both sides of the
House to a conference in
Teheran seems certain to fail.
The conference, which begins
on June 2, js being held to
revue U.S.-Iran relations over
the last 25 years.
Among those who received
invitations by telephone yesterday was Mr. Tam Dalyell

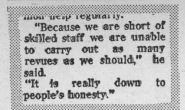

...ion help regularly.

"Because we are short of skilled staff we are unable to carry out as many revues as we should," he said.

"It is really down to people's honesty."

As reported on page one, Mr Kenneth Tynan, the distinguished film and theatre critic, died in California at the weekend at the age of 53. Mr Tynan, who had been ill for some time, achieved notoriery by being the first man to use a four-letter word on television and as the co-author of the erotic review Oh! Calcutta!

Auditions are being held today for parts in the Master of the Rolls' new review, which will be performed in the Old Hall in Lincoln's Inn in October. The show comprises extracts

Cleese revives review

THE hugely successful Secret Policeman's Ball — Amnesty International's 1979 review— is back on the boards next month, with a cast assembled by John Cleese.

107

Poignant history to funeral right

108

MY HUSBAND and I have been rowing like mad. When we came home from a party

A 24-year-old Bootle man who lived in fear of dying, hanged himself after rowing with his wife, a Liverpool inquest was told.

" Mr Jones built a slurry pit and my husband rowed with him over the smell," she said.

no hard feelings. "We were both drinking and rowing but Women's Lib had nothing to do with the breakdown," he declared, adding that he

house. On the day of Mrs Moller's death, the couple rowed over the divorce, and Moller said in court yesterday:

Dolphins row

AN AMERICAN environmentalist has been given a sixmonth suspended sentence by a Japanese court for preventing fishermen from catching 250 dolphins in a case that aroused world-wide interest.

109

But in the formal sur-
roundings of the Albert
Hall, with Carl Davis's
bluntly satyrical music,
she has plainly bitten off
more than even her capa-

and finally, Nijinsky was reviled
for doing unspeakable things to
himself with his veil, as he danced
Debussy's music, pursued by his
attendant nymphs and satires. A

110

in July and August there is
always a seasonable rise in
jobs in seaside towns, with
vacancies for such menial
jobs as deck-chair attendants
and street photographers.

111

An article in the Soviet writers Union newspaper liter-
arary gazette said the dancer
had been beseiged by anti-
Soviet elements offering him
" mountains of gold and a sea
of free whisky."

Gunmen
sieze
British
bankers

"It's a dreadful place—but quite honestly I was releived at what I found after the things I had heard." he said. "There's

Between times Arsenal's penalty box was under seige, as the League champions battled with skill, determination and at times fury in an effort to close the gap.

112

The manner of approach of the council's official, by telephone, with peremtory order to remove the posters by noon tomorrow smattered of intimidation, particularly in addressing a lady.

113

and on the M6 there was a six-mile gridlock that effectively brought all traffic to a standstill. Only after two

114

work in longhand. Visitors to the House of Commons on a Thursday afternoon would sometimes be taken to the press gallery library and be shown a somnambulant figure recumbent in a deep armchair.

115

FREE to kind home, young spade female cat. grey and ginger; abandoned by owners. Tel. 222009.   n263545

116

THE WEATHER in the Straights of Dover is traditionally stormy - even in the best of summers.

the sculptor lived in straightened circumstances near London until 1957, when he achieved success-

Having received six of the best, the boy straitened up and wept unashamedly, clutching his bottom with both hands.

Then came two men in white coats and put a straight-jacket on me so I could not move.

117

De Lorean, who created the stylistic De Lorean sports car, was arrested yesterday at Los Angeles international airport as he arrived to pick up 220 pounds of cocaine valued at £14 million the FBI said.

118

HE EXPECTS ANY DAY TO BE SUMMONSED TO BUCKINGHAM PALACE TO RECEIVE HIS GONG FROM THE QUEEN

119

Thieves take Silk

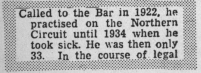

Called to the Bar in 1922, he practised on the Northern Circuit until 1934 when he took sick. He was then only 33. In the course of legal

120

Mr Carter, an ambulanceman from Eastbourne, started queueing outside Selfridge's 14 days ago, armed with sleeping bag and thermal blankets.

BEFORE setting out, they invested in large quantities of thermal underwear, intended to keep out the fierce Arctic winds. Above

121

THEY call it the generation of the Kalashnikov, the young people of Beirut now in their early twenties who grew up touting machine guns. They were hurtled abruptly and brutally into adulthood during the civil

tne villagers had become a
misery. The PLO quite literally took over the whole
area. They paraded the
streets touting their guns,
shooting into the air, and
generally frightening the life
out of all of us.

122

All who knew her would unhesitatingly
have described Jessie Matthews as an old
trooper. She had a fine clear voice, with

123

its right place. A thousand ships with a
thousand cargoes are being unladen every
week. And not only is each package of this

124

now he is sitting on the
opposition front bench
again, dreaming he was
back in office.

125

MUCH THE best part of this
week was wiled away yesterday morning, aloft on the
Collegiate Church of St Peter
in Westminster. This edifice,
better if not wholly accurately known as Westminster
Abbey, has been girded for
eight years now by a raft of

126

but now, unfortunately, the Scotch Whiskey distillers are feeling the cold draught of reality blowing up the glens. Demand has slumped and there is competition even from Japan.

127

One highly intelligent girl with reading problems who I have known from childhood (she is now working for a PhD.)

Herr Maywald, whom the judge said was not a hater of Jews, was convicted of selecting 320 Jews in the Jungfernhof camp near Riga for shooting on February 5, 1942.

mann's wife Clara. She was 14 years older than him (Brahms's mother was 17 years older than his father), and when Schumann became deranged Brahms and Clara became inseparable

Amin's divorces leave him with only one official wife, Medina whom he claims was given to him in 1971.

Disc jockey Jimmy Young, who Mrs. Thatcher has described as "my favourite interviewer" gets an OBE. Mr Michael

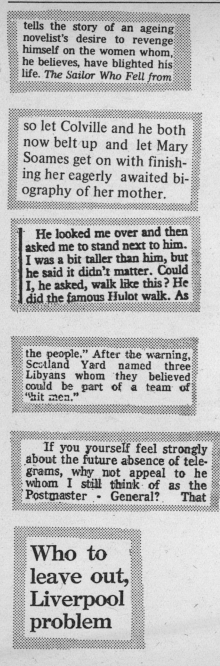

tells the story of an ageing
novelist's desire to revenge
himself on the women whom,
he believes, have blighted his
life. *The Sailor Who Fell from*

so let Colville and he both
now belt up and let Mary
Soames get on with finishing her eagerly awaited bi-
ography of her mother.

He looked me over and then
asked me to stand next to him.
I was a bit taller than him, but
he said it didn't matter. Could
I, he asked, walk like this? He
did the famous Hulot walk. As

the people." After the warning,
Scotland Yard named three
Libyans whom they believed
could be part of a team of
"hit men."

If you yourself feel strongly
about the future absence of tele-
grams, why not appeal to he
whom I still think of as the
Postmaster - General? That

Who to leave out, Liverpool problem

Research proved it had at one time belonged to Sir Samuel Morton Peto, then M P for Norwich and it was possibly passed to him by Edward Smith Stanley, Earl of Derby, who shared the same interest as him in aviaries.

It is anathema both to the Russians and we that such events might happen.

solicitor listening intently. The two men who Mr Smith had earlier accused of being involved in his daughter's murder in a short outburst, Dr Arnot and M. Jaques Texier, sat impassively throughout the summing-up.

At the end of the interview he slowly rose to his feet and said, gravely, 'Between you and I, I can tell you she is absolutely crazy about you and he.' But I chose to

Mrs Cartland added, 'The one thing that makes you and I individuals is our brains.' She then pressed a jar of honey on me, which I accepted grate-

Philip Rastelli, the man whom the police intelligence department thinks has assumed control, is still serving the rest of a 10-year prison sentence imposed in 1977 for extortion.

THE PICCADILLY Undergound Line to Heathrow is a boon to we baboons who fly a lot.

A magician conjured up three fire engines yesterday, when he triggered an automatic smoke alarm during a fire trick at the Viking Hotel, York. The entertainer, who the hotel refused to name, was "a little embarrassed."

In the long run, just whom do they think they are fooling? Gradually the word spreads. Yet part of the damage is well-nigh irreparable. One cannot

The father of the British nurse, Miss Helen Smith, yesterday named the man whom he believes murdered his daughter in Saudi Arabia 27 months ago.

during the first few days of the Senate hearings when Joseph McCarthy charged the Secretary of the Army, Robert T. Stevens, with trying to blackmail he and his loyal staff.

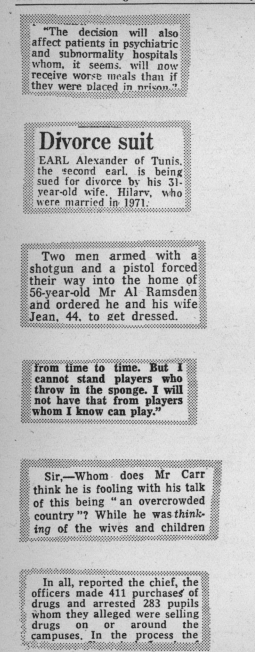

"The decision will also affect patients in psychiatric and subnormality hospitals whom, it seems, will now receive worse meals than if they were placed in prison."

Divorce suit

EARL Alexander of Tunis, the second earl, is being sued for divorce by his 31-year-old wife. Hilary, who were married in 1971.

Two men armed with a shotgun and a pistol forced their way into the home of 56-year-old Mr Al Ramsden and ordered he and his wife Jean, 44, to get dressed.

from time to time. But I cannot stand players who throw in the sponge. I will not have that from players whom I know can play."

Sir,—Whom does Mr Carr think he is fooling with his talk of this being " an overcrowded country "? While he was *thinking* of the wives and children

In all, reported the chief, the officers made 411 purchases of drugs and arrested 283 pupils whom they alleged were selling drugs on or around the campuses. In the process the

Sir Peter has also been in touch with Mrs Barbara Stonehouse whom friends say is now a frightened woman.

The theory that Mr Stone.

The police were seeking a man who was thought to be trying to travel to India, and whom they hoped could help with their inquiries.

gic to emerge as our leading pop poet. Linton Kwesi Johnson — who Clarke much admires — is obviously working in a similar field, but

rilla in a movie directed by Fritz Lang, himself an expatriate whom she thought would be kind to her. But she burned her stockings with the machine-gun. was bullied

Us from the working class have had to make it totally on our own. If I'd had a proper education and gone to university, would I ever have become editor of the *Daily Express*?

128

1 AGORAPHOBIA The Greek word for a fear of open spaces; a form of mental illness whose sufferers are afraid of going out from their home. It comes from the Greek words *agora*, a meeting-place, or market-place, and *phobia*, fear. But Greek words are not to be trifled with by our modern poor spellers: 'aggrophobia' would be fear of aggression; 'agro-phobia', a fear of open fields (as would be 'agriphobia' – cf. 'agriculture') and 'agraphobia', the fear of the unwritten. There are, of course, no such words, but newspapermen nevertheless keep inventing them.

2 ALLEGORY/ANALOGY Both words describe a form of comparison: 'allegory', from Greek *allos*, other, and *agoreuo*, to speak: a way of describing, or speaking of, one subject in terms of another; 'analogy', from Greek *analogia*, *ana*, other, and *logos*, ratio, proportion. The parables (from *para*, beside, and *ballo*, to throw) in the Scriptures contain both allegory and analogy.

3 AMPUTATION/DECAPITATION Amputation: from Latin *am(b)*, about, + *putare*, to prune, lop: the cutting off a limb. Decapitation: from Latin *de* + *caput* (*capit-*), applies only to the removal of the head.

4 ANTE/ANTI The first is Latin for 'before', and the second means 'against'. An ante-natal clinic is a place where women receive attention before they give birth to their babies. An anti-natal one, if there were such a thing, would be a clinic giving advice about contraception. The Americans show rare discrimination by differentiating between the two words in pronunciation: 'an-tee' and 'ant-eye', respectively – which is all the more surprising as they fail to distinguish between 'missal' and 'missile'.

5 ANTICIPATE/EXPECT From Latin *anticipare*, to take (an action) before; or, as the OED says, 'To take up or deal with (a thing), or perform (an action) before another person . . . has had time to act . . . to observe or practise in advance of the due date'. It does not mean, as many speakers and writers seem to think, the same as 'expect'.

6 APPOINTED AS A common solecism. 'Last year he was appointed as MP for Louth', or 'She was elected as lady president of the students' union.' No. He was appointed as an ordinary citizen; she as a student. They became MP or president, respectively, only *after* their election.

7 ASSIDUOUS/ACIDULOUS 'Assiduous': from Latin *assidere*, to sit by, to be in constant attendance; 'acidulous': from L. *acidulus*, sourish, slightly sour. 'Aciduous' is an accidental but delightful coinage.

8 ASTRONAUTS/COSMONAUTS The first name applies to American space travellers, the second to Russian ones.

9 ASTRONOMICAL From Greek *astron*, star, and *nomos*, law, rule; and therefore a word relating to things up on high.

10 BALMY/BARMY 'Balmy': mild, deliciously fragrant, soothing and refreshing: from balsam, a tree that gave forth a healing and sweet-smelling resin: 'Ewiry blome . . . opynt & spred thair balmy leves . . .' wrote William Dunbar in The Goldyn Targe (c 1500). 'Barmy': the present meaning is 'amiably and mildly mad, potty, scatty', as in 'I must have been barmy to say that.' It comes from 'barm', meaning froth, such as 'barmy ale', hence 'barmy-brained' = frothy, windy, bubblingly empty-headed.

11 BATE/BAIT 'Bated' means diminished, reduced, abated. The term 'with bated breath' has survived because Shakespeare uses it in The Merchant of Venice: 'With bated breath and whispering humbleness, say this.' Breath used as a bait is an interesting absurdity.

12 BEATIFICATION/BEAUTIFICATION In the Roman Church, the action of rendering someone blessed, that is, one step before complete canonisation, or sainthood. It is not, as some newspapermen and broadcasters seem to think, a form of cosmetic treatment.

13 BEQUEATHING/'BEQUESTING' The word for making a bequest is now 'bequeathing', though 'bequesting' was sometimes used in the eighteenth century and earlier.

14 BLANCH/BLENCH The two are not interchangeable, but a person who has just had a fright might do both. He could 'blanch', that is his face may be drained of its colour (old French, blanchir, to whiten), while also 'blenching', i.e. flinch, quail or give a sudden start with fear or shock (from old English blencan, which also gave us the verb 'to blink').

15 BLOND/BLONDE Fair-haired men are blond, women are blonde; the latter described as 'blondes', the former as 'blond men', not 'blonds'.

16 BOOM/BOON A boom, says the OED, is 'a start of commercial activity, as when a new book, the shares of a commercial undertaking, or the like, "go off" with a "boom"; a rapid advance in prices; a sudden bound in activity in any business or speculation'. 'Boon', on the other hand, comes from various old Norse, middle English and old English words like bon, bowne, ben for a prayer – granting a boon, a favour conferred or prayer answered (compare 'benison').

17 BOTTLENECK According to the OED supplement (1972), 'bottleneck', in the sense of something obstructing the flow of, perhaps, industrial production, was first used by an imaginative writer on the Observer in 1928. Over-use has, however, made it into a boring cliché. What is more, it is used with disregard for its meaning; for a 'big' bottleneck would increase the flow rather than retard it.

18 CENT(E)RING AROUND An absurd impossibility. One may as well say that the equator 'centres around' the earth.

19 CHARTED/CHARTERED Charted rocks are those which appear on charts; chartered liners are hired from their owners.

20 CHEAPEN/MAKE CHEAPER Cheapening is a matter of taste. For example, an opera star may cheapen himself by accepting a subsidy from a tobacco company – without making himself cheaper by reducing his fee. It is more a convention of usage than a hard-and-fast rule.

21 COLLIDING WITH/RUNNING INTO Colliding comes from the Latin word *collidere*, to strike or clash together – that is, a collision between two bodies or objects moving towards each other. It is therefore inaccurate to say that a car 'collided with a wall' unless the wall came to meet the car. However, when a newspaper report says 'a car collided with a pedestrian' the intention is to avoid the impression that blame is being apportioned, as would be the case if it said 'a car ran into a pedestrian'. The pedestrian could have run into the car.

22 COLOSSEUM/COLISEUM From the neuter form of the adjective *colosseus*, later adapted into medieval Latin, *coliseum*, Italian *coliseo*, French *colisée*, all meaning gigantic, colossal. Both spellings are therefore correct, but the Colosseum (the amphitheatre of Vespasian) is in Rome, and the Coliseum Theatre in St Martin's Lane, London WC2.

23 COMPRISE/COMPROMISE The first means to consist of; the second, to implicate in some dishonourable, shameful (or now sexual) manner.

24 COSTLY/COSTIVE People never tire of seeking euphemisms for spending a lot of money. 'Dear' labours under a double meaning ('You're the Dearest Girl in Town', sang Dr Arne in the middle of the eighteenth century to a London prostitute); which is why some prefer 'expensive' as a more genteel alternative. 'Costive', however, is not the same as 'expensive', in spite of the now fashionable '-ive' ending. It comes from old French *costive*, which itself is a contraction of the Latin *constipatus*, constipated.

25 COWBOYS AND (SOUTH AMERICAN) INDIANS Cowboy operators, or simply cowboys, are unscrupulous, dishonest, fly-by-night merchants who may perform some promised service badly (and in some cases not at all), take the money and disappear. That is the modern jargon-meaning of the word, derived from the wild young men of the nineteenth-century American west. Not all countries subscribe to this usage. I once commented on an example of wildly reckless driving on the streets of Buenos Aires with the words 'He's driving like a cowboy – or should I say *gaucho*?' but was told by my Argentinian host that calling someone a gaucho is to pay him a compliment. To behave like a gaucho is to display gentlemanly, almost knightly, qualities.

26 COWORKERS AND COPRODUCERS The useful prefix 'co-', from the Latin preposition *com* (which, when used as a separate word, was written *cum*, with) denotes co-operation. The hyphen is often more important than writers realise; 'coworkers' (especially when split 'cow-orkers' across two lines) and 'coproducers' not only have an unfamiliar look about them but can also suggest cows and dung respectively (the Greek prefix copro-, from copros=dung).

27 CREDIBILITY/CREDULITY Credere, to believe, in Latin. He who has credibility is to be believed; but he who is credulous is ready or disposed to believe.

28 CUTTING A SWATHE An archaism kept alive only by its use as a news cliché. Its real meaning is the path cut by a single sweep of a mower's scythe.

29 DECIMATE When Roman soldiers showed signs of becoming unruly or rebellious, their commanders would put to death one man in ten, so as to persuade the rest to behave themselves. But 'decimate' is now used for any drastic reduction, which some say is an example of legitimate change in usage. But as it so patently comes from the Latin word for 'ten', resistance to the change is to be applauded.

30 DELIRIOUS/DELIRIUM From Latin deliro, deranged, out of the straight, which in turn comes from de + lira, a furrow. In its medical application it means an acute disorder relating to brain disease, illusion and disorientation caused by certain diseases or high body temperature. But that doesn't bother those who consider it the standard abbreviation for the cliché 'deliriously happy'.

31 DESERTS/DESSERTS The confusion between what we eat and what we deserve is probably caused by the fact that both are pronounced in the same way.

32 DIRECT/DIRECTLY 'Direct' = by the shortest route; 'directly' = at once. Some think that to add '-ly' to a word makes it more polite, and that adverbs are posher than mere adjectives.

33 DISCOMFORT/DISCOMFITURE The second is not an elegant synonym of the first: the one is physical discomfort, the other refers to embarrassment – to be routed, put to flight or otherwise disconcerted. When Mr Walter Annenberg became the United States ambassador to Britain, he was asked by the Queen where he was living. He replied, 'In the embassy, ma'am, subject to a certain amount of discomfiture owing to the necessity for refurbishment.' As that wise American, Morton Cooper, said: 'Giving the English language to the Americans is like giving sex to small children. They know it's important but they don't know what the hell to do with it.'

34 DISSOLUTION/DISILLUSION One would think few people with access to print could confuse the processes of being dissolved and disenchanted, respectively.

35 DRIVING/DRIVING In her car, or by her nagging?

36 DROOLING/DRULING (OVER) To slaver, salivate with excessive longing or appreciation for something that – literally or figuratively – stimulates the appetite. It is related to 'drivel', an alternative form of 'dribble'. When writers spell it 'drule' they are (perhaps accidentally) reviving an archaic spelling; but the modern form is 'drool'.

37 DYE/DIE Both 'dyeing' (changing the colour of hair, material, etc.) and 'dying' (ceasing to live) come from Nordic words: 'dyeing' from Anglo-Saxon *deagan*, from *deag*, colour; and 'dying' from various related Danish, Frisian or Icelandic forms like *deya*, leading to Anglo-Saxon 'dead', German *tot*, etc. Further confusion is caused by 'die', the singular of 'dice' (cubes with letters or symbols embossed on their faces), which comes from Latin *datum*, something given, or laid on the table, possibly in a game of chance. Archaic spelling often confuses all three forms, but that is no excuse for getting it wrong.

38 DYED IN THE WOOL/DIED IN THE WOOL Material made from dyed wool, not dyed as a made-up garment; hence the comparison to something or somebody imbued through and through with a certain quality, such as a 'dyed-in-the-wool conservative'. 'Died in the wool' is often erroneously used by journalists. Death from 'hyperthermia', perhaps? (See Number 58.)

39 EFFETE/EFFEMINATE Contrary to popular belief, the two are not interchangeable, nor is the first a contraction of the second. Critics love using 'effete' to mean weak, intellectually exhausted, limp-wristed, because the word *looks* as if it should mean these things. However, femininity (or at any rate femaleness) does come into it. 'Effete' comes from the Latin adverb *effetus*, that which has brought forth young, hence, worn out by child-bearing: ex, out; and *fetus*, breeding. In other words, clapped out. Mrs Malaprop would have loved this one.

40 ENERVATING From e + *nervus* – deprived of sinew, and therefore weak and deficient of force. But what could this writer have meant? Pleasantly nerve-tingling, perhaps?

41 ENORMITY/ENORMOUSNESS An 'enormity' is a breach of the law or of morality, something grossly improper, wicked, deformed or outrageous, from Latin e, out of, and *norma*, square, pattern. This also provided the origin of 'enormousness' in size; but the two words have had separate meanings for many centuries, so it is silly to start confusing them now.

42 EVACUATE This is a transitive verb: you evacuate something or somebody. Children were evacuated during the Second World War (and described as 'evacuees'). Intransitive use suggests only the bowels.

43 EXACT/EXTRACT The two verbs are often confused. To 'exact' vengeance, from Latin ex-, out, + *agere*, to drive; but to 'extract' a tooth, confession, etc., from ex- + *trahere*, to draw.

44 EXERCISE/EXORCISE 'Exercise': a difficult word to define, but various dictionaries suggest 'The action of employing a certain organ, faculty or power in its appropriate manner', etc. On its own, 'exercise', verb and noun, is a shortened way of saying 'physical exercise', or mild gymnastic activity. 'Exorcise', from the Greek exorkiso, means to expel or drive out supposed demons, devils or evil spirits.

45 FLAUNT/FLOUT You 'flaunt', or show off, your wealth; but flout authority. 'Flaunting' is of unknown origin, with a possible suggestion of waving flags or banners. 'Flouting', to express contempt, mock, jeer, insultingly ignore, etc., is probably connected with flute-playing: the Dutch word fluiten means both fluting and mocking.

46 FLOUNDER/FOUNDER A washed-up whale (or even a flounder) may 'flounder', that is, struggle and flap about – desperately wishing it could 'founder' like a ship; for 'foundering' means sinking to the bottom (from Latin fundus, the bottom, or fundament).

47 FORBIDDEN TO/PREVENTED FROM A common confusion of prepositions.

48 FORCEFULLY/FORCIBLY Two words that are almost the same, although over the years there has arisen an interesting distinction between them. A 'forceful' speaker or writer is one who makes his points cogently, effectively and with energy; but a 'forcible' act is now almost always physical and probably violent. I doubt whether the writer of this letter was really taken by the scruff of the neck and dragged back to Oxford.

49 FORMER/ONE-TIME 'One-time' is a translation of the German einmalig (Es war einmal = once upon a time) – and a clumsy one at that, for a 'one-time lover' may be one who managed to love only once.

50 GAOL/JAIL A prison; a place or building for the confinement of persons accused or convicted of an offence. The two spellings have the same pronunciation and have come down to us from much the same origins. The 'gaol' form has survived only because that is how the word is written in old laws. Newspapers for some reason seem to prefer it – perhaps so that compositors can misspell it 'goal'. The middle English spelling was gayhole, which could lead to some interesting if spurious etymologies.

51 GET ONTO/GET ON TO The first is geographical, the second means 'get in touch with'.

52 GEYSERS/GEEZERS The only thing the two words share is the pronunciation. A 'geyser' (from an Icelandic word geysir, a hot spring) is a machine for heating water in the bathroom or kitchen. A 'geezer' is an old person, usually an old man, derisively described; from gyser, gysour, guiser, a word existing in many spelling since the fifteenth century and meaning a mummer, masquerader, one who dresses in unusual clothes.

53 GREENGROCER'S APOSTROPHE The English never were the 'nation of shopkeepers' Napoleon's propagandists declared them to be, but the 'greengrocer's apostrophe' is ALIVE AND WELL← in the columns of English newspapers. Not that others don't misuse the apostrophe: they are merely less public about it, and do not daily advertise their wares by painting their prices on shop-windows in white paint. It is an admirable form of folk art, the letters sometimes decoratively written, mirror fashion, on the inside of the glass. But greengrocers labour under a misapprehension about the function of the apostrophe, thinking that it is needed to turn a singular noun into the plural. It has several uses, including the indication of possessives ('the nation's resolve') or that letters have been omitted ('isn't'), and to a limited degree can indicate the plural (as in 'do's and don't's'); but the greengrocer's frequent assertion that tomatoes becomes 'tomato's', potatoes 'potato's' and greens 'green's' is not supported by grammatical facts. There is occasionally some agitation in the correspondence columns of newspapers from people who advocate the abolition of the apostrophe, as the Germans have already done (*Bachs Werke*). The idea was put forward long ago by George Bernard Shaw, who had some of his works printed without apostrophes. But readers complained that they could not tell the difference between 'can't' and 'cant', 'she'll' and 'shell', 'he'll' and 'hell' or 'we'll' and 'well'. Modern ignorance about apostrophes must be put down to bad teaching. (There is, indeed, a journal for educationists which is published under the proud masthead *Teachers World*.) 'Nigger's out', read a mural scrawl in Liverpool. Someone wrote underneath: 'When's he coming back?'

54 HAIR'S BREADTH/HARE'S BREATH The confusion is made a little more understandable by the fact that the word 'breadth' has in recent years been almost supplanted by 'width' when describing physical distance; and even in figurative use ('his breadth of artistic imagination') its awkwardness is apparent, especially when spoken. In the nineteenth century related words like 'breadthen', 'breadthways' and 'breadthless' were still common. See also Number 11.

55 HIATUS/HICCUP Hiatus comes from the Latin *hiare*, to gape. It means a gap; not a mishap, snag, hold-up or 'hiccup'. The music critic who wrote, 'There was a slight hiatus in the wind section when the first oboe played a B flat instead of a natural', intended to tell his readers that the note was wrong, not missing.

56 HOARDS/HORDES Hoard comes from the old Saxon word *hord*, treasure, and is often confused with 'horde', a multitude such as a tribe travelling together and often resorting to plunder as it travels. It comes from various Eastern languages, *orda*, *ordi*, *ordu* and *urdu* (the last meaning a camp), denoting a horde, clan, crowd or troop. The Polish word is *horda*, the Russian *orda* ('Hordes of Russian tanks invading Hungary') is a precise use of the word; but many writers consider – wrongly – that the spelling is interchangeable.

57 HUNG/HANGED Beef, game and pictures are 'hung', persons are (in some countries) 'hanged'. When people regrettably commit suicide by hanging, they are said to have 'hanged', not 'hung', themselves. The press usually gets it wrong. When in doubt, ask yourself: Do I say, 'Well, I'm hung!' or 'Well, I'm hanged!'?

58 HYPER/HYPO When a poor speller gets a long English word wrong, he may excuse himself by saying, 'Oh, but you *know* what I mean' – and the odd wrong letter or two may indeed make little difference. But he cannot afford to treat Greek prefixes in such a cavalier manner. *Hypo* denotes a deficiency, a lack of something or too little; *hyper*, the opposite, i.e. too much, too big or abnormally increased. It is especially important for doctors to know the difference.

59 IMMIGRANT/EMIGRANT An immigrant is an emigrant who has already arrived (and possibly settled) in his new country; emigrant, a person who is leaving or about to leave his own country – in the hope of becoming an immigrant elsewhere. The distinction comes from the Latin prefix e- meaning out and im- meaning in, both in conjunction with *migrare*, to migrate. Americans tend to use 'immigrate' for both. If unsure, use 'migrant' and hedge your bets.

60 INFECTED/INFESTED The difference seems to be a matter of size: we are infected with germs and viruses so small that only a microscope can detect them; infestation with rats, mice, lice, fleas, worms, beetles or terrorists is only too visibly obvious.

61 INIMICAL/'INIMICABLE' There is at present no such word as 'inimicable', though many people think there should be one. If they persevere long enough they will get their way. That is how language changes, for dictionaries soon capitulate to verbal hijackers.

62 IRREPARABLE/IRREVERSIBLE It is sometimes possible to 'repair' damage, never to 'reverse' it. The distressing news stories about 'irreversible brain damage' are therefore absurd.

63 JINKS/JINX 'Jinking' is one of the many old euphemisms for copulating; 'high jinks' was an early eighteenth-century dice game which combined gaming with drinking – hence possibly general connotations of abandoned, alcoholic frolics. In football (both of the round ball and oval ball kind) a 'jinking' player, or 'jinker', is one who can quickly change direction with a suitably agile movement of the hips. A 'jinx' is something (more rarely somebody) that brings bad luck or failure on a project or enterprise – or at any rate is thought to signify a bad omen. Shakespeare's *Macbeth* is said by actors to be a jinx play.

64 KNIGHTED/BENIGHTED A man 'benighted' is one overtaken by darkness – moral, intellectual, spiritual or (rarely nowadays) actual. It has nothing to do with being knighted by the Queen. The occasional example of men going to Buckingham Palace to be 'benighted' is at best a bad pun and at worst a good malapropism.

65 LARGE/LARGELY The first means big, great etc.; 'largely' is, in that sense, not only no improvement but an absurdity, used by those who feel it is somehow more genteel with the '-ly' ending: 'How are you?' 'Very nicely, thank you.' See 'direct/directly' (Number 32). 'Largely' means to a great extent, widely, extensively.

66 LAY/LIE 'Lay' is transitive: you lay something or somebody. 'Now I lay me down to sleep.' That which has been laid 'lies'. The confusion is compounded by well-established dialect and slang usage, which has in some cases been perpetuated by such things as (in Britain) the 'layby' at the side of roads, which is really a 'bay' in which traffic 'lies' and should therefore be called a 'lie-bay', though the international word 'parking' is now superseding 'layby'. 'Layabouts' are also misnamed, as they are idle people who 'lie about', and who may even be 'lie-abeds' – a nice, old-fashioned word well worth reviving. Such confusions are especially jarring when they occur in over-elaborate, stilted language.

67 LEGENDARY/FAMOUS Literally, legendary means what is read, from Latin *legere*, to read; and therefore thought to have been invented. Later it came to mean fictional, non-historical. In modern journalistic usage it merely means famous. See also FAMED←.

68 LIMP/LIMPID Contrary to popular belief (shared by some music critics), the two words do not mean the same thing. 'Limp' means wanting in firmness or stiffness (and, of course, an uneven gait) and is of obscure origin, says the *OED*. 'Limpid' comes from Latin *limpidus*, or *limpha*, a clear liquid, and means transparent, translucent and clear.

69 LIQUIDISED/LIQUIDATED In modern usage, food mixed with liquids in an electric kitchen utensil called a 'liquidiser' is 'liquidised'. Repressive governments or terrorist organisations 'liquidate' their opponents, i.e. murder them. Like so many terms of terror and repression, this was of Russian origin and began as a euphemism, from Russian *liquidirovat* (itself from the German Marxist word *liquidisieren*) meaning to wind up, abolish, put an end to, also used when putting firms out of business. But it soon became clear that what Stalin was doing to the people he was 'liquidating' was murdering them. See WINDING UP←.

70 LOTH/LOATH/LOATHE 'Loth' and 'loath' – the dictionaries give both adjectival forms – mean unwilling, or reluctant, and have a hard 'th' sound. 'Loathe' is a verb meaning to feel hatred or strong dislike, and has a soft 'th' ending. 'Loth' is therefore to be preferred to 'loathe'. It not only helps to avoid confusion but is also enshrined in a beautiful piece of music by John Dowland, 'Loth to Depart'.

71 MEMENTO(E)S/EPHEMERA There seems to be a growing belief that mementos are 'momentos', and thus even more short-lived than 'ephemera'. The latter (which include such throw-away objects as bus tickets, advertising leaflets, etc.) get their name from the Greek word *ephemeros*, lasting a day. 'Mementos' (from the Latin imperative of *meminisse*, to remember) should last for ever, not, as some writers think, a mere moment.

72 METAL/METTLE Both come from *metallum*, the Latin word for mine, quarry or the substance obtained from mining or quarrying. Until English spelling settled down into some kind of standardisation in the early nineteenth century, the two spellings were interchangeable, but eventually the meanings as well as the spellings divided into 'metal' for the substance and 'mettle' for the figurative description of a man's (or perhaps also a horse's) qualities of spirit, vigour, etc. Unfortunately the present-day tendency to revert to a single spelling stems less from historical nicety than ignorance or carelessness.

73 METEOROLOGICAL (OFFICE) From Greek *meta* = beyond, *aeiro* = to raise: a clumsy and unattractive word at the best of times, but with the additional disadvantage that it is now associated more with the weather than meteors. Its seven syllables are more than some spellers and radio speakers can cope with, and the latter often reduce them to 'meaty-logical' or even 'meat-orogical'. So why not 'Met Office', a usage which was found perfectly acceptable in the Second World War? Or even 'Weather Office'?

74 MILITATE/MITIGATE To 'militate', which requires 'against' in its use, means to conflict, or be inconsistent with something; from Latin *militare*, to fight, or engage in conflict. To 'mitigate' something is to soften it, render it milder and less hostile; from Latin *mitis*, mild. The two words have almost opposite meanings, yet are often used as if they meant the same thing.

75 MILLIONS, BILLIONS, TRILLIONS, ZILLIONS AND MILLIARDS This is a subject on which the Americans and the British are unable to agree. An American 'billion' is 1,000,000,000 that is, a thousand millions. The English call this a 'milliard' (as do the Germans and the French), and a million millions (1,000,000,000,000) a billion. A 'trillion' is the third power of a million, or a million billions, but in France and parts of the USA this is a thousand billions, i.e. an English 'billion'. The terminology goes back to c 1484, and can be adapted almost indefinitely, from 'quadrillions' to 'nonillions' and even 'zillions'. The confusion is made worse by the fact that some British people have adopted the American form, possibly because they are unaware that there is a difference, or think the Americans must be right as they have so much more money. The American form will, no doubt, prevail eventually. Meanwhile it is better to specify the amount in numerals, so as to avoid confusing your bank manager; or else restrict the terms to facetious usage, as in Scouse:* 'There wuz millyins of rats runnin' all over the kitchen', which simply means 'rather more than I was able to count'.

76 MINUSCULE/'MINISCULE' A 'minuscule' is something very small, or, in printing, the old name for a lower-case or small letter (i.e. not a capital). We are now so used to the prefix 'mini' that we almost always misspell it. There is no such word as 'miniscule' – though a Liverpool schoolchild once defined it as a 'kindergarten'.

77 MYSELF Writers who are not sure about their cases, whether to use 'I' or 'me', are likely to play safe by opting for the neutral but too emphatic 'myself'. They are vaguely aware that 'me' (as in 'Who's there?' 'It's me') is too informal when written rather than spoken, but find the first person singular stiltedly formal. This is especially common when comparisons are being made: rather than write 'he looks like my wife and me' (which is, of course, correct but may *sound* vulgar to writers uncertain about grammar) they put '. . . like my wife and myself'; 'he gave it to my wife and myself', etc. English is a fruitful language for alternatives, but with 'I', 'me' and 'myself' one gets it either right or wrong. See also Number 128 for similar troubles with 'who' and 'whom'.

78 NAVAL/NAVEL Is it possible some people don't know the difference?

79 NOISOME/NOISY The first is not an elegant alternative to the second. Many pop musicians are both noisome and noisy, but those who wash themselves may be merely noisy. There are some connections between 'noise', 'nausea', 'noxiousness' and even the human 'nose'; but modern usage dictates that what is *noisy* may offend the ear, whereas the *noisome* affects the nose.

80 THE NON-SEXIST PLURAL CONFUSION This comes about when a writer, anxious not to incur the displeasure of feminists, avoids the use of the all-embracing 'he', decides that 'he or she' would be too clumsy and therefore resorts to the non-committal but ungrammatical 'they'. There are enough plural confusions in English – most of them perfectly avoidable by rephrasing – without the needless addition of non-sexist ones.

81 ON THE FLOOR/ON THE GROUND Dimly aware, perhaps, that the phrase 'on the ground' has become a media cliché relating to politics

*Lern yorself Scouse, ed. Spiegl, Scouse Press, Liverpool.

('he has much support on the ground'), journalists use 'floor' where 'ground' is the proper word. Rooms have floors, but in the open air the firm basis for walking on is the ground. When the Fleet Street Bible is eventually written, Genesis 3,9 will read: 'The voice of thy brother's blood crieth unto me from the floor.'

82 ORDINANCE/ORDNANCE Although both words go back to the same origins, the first spelling is now applied to an order, the second to a machine for discharging a projectile or missile. Notice also the unconventional substitution of 'intermediary' for 'intermediate'.

83 OVERLOOK/OVERSEE You may 'oversee' someone to make sure he does not make a mistakes. Then, if he does err, his errors may be 'overlooked' and forgiven: noticed but not necessarily mentioned. The windows of a house may 'overlook' a river. The distinctions are part of the idiomatic charm of the English language. Any attempts to extinguish them should be resisted.

84 PALATE/PALETTE/PALLET Newspaper people seem to be unsure whether they lick it, mix paint on it, or sleep on it. 'Palate': the roof of the mouth, from Latin *palatum*. 'Palette': from Latin, *pala*, a shovel (diminutive, *paletta*); but if you were to go into a shop in Italy and ask for a *paletta*, you would be given a flat spoon or else a bricklayer's trowel. An artist would demand a *tavolozza* (diminutive of *tavola*, a table) for mixing his paints. As for 'pallet' – it appears that when the distinguished wine correspondent of a national paper has to make an important decision about a vintage, she sleeps on it (though perhaps the blame lies with a sub-editor or compositor). 'Pallet' meaning a rude mattress, comes from Latin *palea*, chaff, probably via the French *paille*, straw, with which it would be filled.

85 PANDER TO/CATER FOR You 'pander *to*' but 'cater *for*' something or somebody.

86 PEDAL/PEDDLE A person who sells, or peddles, goods in a small way is a pedlar, or peddler – often an itinerant one. The OED says the etymology is uncertain but I suggest a connexion with the German *Bettler*, a beggar. *Pedalis* is Latin for anything pertaining to the foot – hence the pedals of a bicycle, an organ, etc. ('foot pedal' is therefore a tautology). Cyclists have become known as 'pedallers', and their action as 'pedalling'; hence the confusion.

87 PENINSULA/PENINSULAR The first is the noun, the second, the adjective.

88 PENURY According to some newsmen, a favourite place where artists take up residence. But the dictionaries tell us that it comes from the Latin *penuria*, poverty, want, and is the condition of being destitute.

89 PER ANNUM/PER ANUM The one means by the year, the other, by the anus (as when taking medication). Increments 'per anum', as in the cutting shown, would make outgoing payments into 'excrements'.

90 PLAYING (THE PALLADIUM) Showbusiness jargon meaning 'playing *at*' (the Palladium Theatre). Here an actor played both Vanya and Parolles, as well as the part of Staines Town Hall and some unnamed swimming-baths. 'Playing the piano' – yes; 'playing the Albert Hall' – no.

91 PORING/POURING You look fixedly, intently and with close attention at something, such as a book – that is, you 'pore' over it (origin obscure); but 'pouring' refers only to liquids.

92 PREMIER/PREMIÈRE These unnecessary French imports mean 'prime minister' and 'first performance', respectively, give or take an accent or two. When in doubt which is which, use English words. Besides, Mrs Thatcher would be more accurately described as a 'première' anyway; but the language has not made provision for women prime ministers or other political leaders, hence facetious coinages such as 'prime ministrette' and 'leaderene'.

93 PRESS/PRESSURE/PRESSURISE You 'press' someone, literally, by squeezing him or exerting some other continuous force against him; or figuratively, by coercing or strongly exhorting him; or 'press on' him something you wish him to have (bearing in mind the danger of being taken too much at your word). To 'pressure', in the same sense, is an absurd and unnecessary Americanism, invented by those who think that making words longer lends extra force to them. 'Pressurise' ('-ize') in that context is worse, except when referring to pressure-cookers or the interior of airliners.

94 PRESTIGIOUS '*Prestige*, you know, I always like to have a pop at; I take it it has never lost its first meaning of conjuring tricks,' writes Edward A. Freeman in *Life and Letters* (1895). The word comes from Latin *praestigium*, a delusion, deception, illusion, a conjuror's trick. The other meaning of the word relates to dazzling, or blinding – as would a conjurer figuratively dazzle his admiring spectators. Thus did it slowly acquire its present meaning, although, of course, there was resistance to it from the purists: Thomas Carlyle called it 'a bad newspaper word'. 'Prestigious' took longer to establish itself, and did not really settle into its present meaning until the press (especially gossip columnists) began to flog it into submission during the 1950s and 60s. Now, and only now, do the big dictionaries admit its new, social climbing sense. But I like to think of a 'prestigious hostess' as one who dazzles her guests by serving cheap sherry from expensive crystal decanters. Even more, I like to juggle with my words so as to find some other way of saying what I want to say without using a doubtful word everyone else is already over-using.

95 PRINCIPAL/PRINCIPLE The difference between the two used to be instilled into one at school with the first principles of spelling – and, in mathematics, the laws of principal and interest. Today's proponents of 'free spelling' have perhaps come to believe that the two are the same.

96 PROCURATION/PROCREATION To 'procreate' children is to beget, or bring them forth, from Latin *procreare*. To 'procure' them is a relatively modern euphemistic abbreviation of the legal term 'procuring for immoral purposes', i.e. prostitution, and is an offence – although it comes from the perfectly respectable Latin word *procurare*. Hence the differences that have arisen between a procurer and the procurator-fiscal, who is a public prosecutor in Scotland.

97 PRODIGY/PROTÉGÉ 'Prodigy': from Latin *prodigiosus*, strange, wonderful, monstrous, extraordinary, enormous; 'a prodigy of nature' being the common description on old fairground advertisements of monsters like two-headed dogs; but also applied to precociously gifted children: '27 Jan., Died my deare son Richard, 5 yeares and 3 days old onely, but at that tender age a prodigy for witt and understanding' – John Evelyn, *Diary* (1658). 'Protégé': from Latin *protegere*, to protect: someone under the protection of another, probably older, richer and more powerful, person, who uses his power or influence to help the person taken under his protection. I suspect that the error in the cutting illustrated was the result of a mishearing, caused by the Americans' reluctance to distinguish between the hard 't' and soft 'd' sounds.

98 PRY/PRISE/PRIZE To 'pry' means to look inquisitively or secretly at someone or something. To 'prise' is to lever something, perhaps a lid, with a tool or coin. To 'prize' something is to regard it with esteem. It is a pity to confuse the three words, each with its clear meaning, but confused they often are, especially by the Americans. Food shops sell a certain kind of meat product whose jar bears the instruction on its lid 'Pry open'. I once received a wooden crate containing a musical instrument with a printed label, 'Prize lid' – which I thought for a moment was an incomplete translation of *Preislied*, known in England as the 'Prize Lied', from *The Mastersingers of* Nuremberg by Wagner.

99 RAZZMATAZZ/RASSMATAZZ/RAZAMATTAZ, etc. A favourite media word, seen in many spellings. Its dictionary meaning is given as 'humbug, old-fashioned or insincere actions', but newsmen use it in the sense of loud and ostentatious rejoicing, boisterous celebration or loudly conspicuous consumption. They probably relate it to 'razzle', as in 'going on the razzle' (and a now defunct magazine) or 'razzle-dazzle', which is excitement, bustle, spree, etc.

100 RECOMPENSE/COMPENSATION One gets compensation for damage, loss or injury, etc., but is recompensed for services rendered.

101 RECORDER/RECORDIST There is such a confusing choice of recorders already that it would be sensible to agree on 'recordist' for one who operates sound-recording apparatus; at present newspapers seem uncertain. Older 'recorders' include: the musical instrument, named after an ancient word for bird-song; the magistrate or judge who has jurisdiction over criminal and civil matters of a city or borough (from the medieval office of recorder, a clerk who recorded council proceedings and who, because he could read and write, occupied a position of privilege and power); and the recording apparatus.

102 REEK/WREAK 'Reek' originally meant to emit smoke, and only later, by extension, came to mean giving off an impure, foul or fetid smell. It comes from a Teutonic word common to various languages, including old English *reocan*. Dutchmen say 'Verboden te rooken' and the Germans 'Rauchen verboten'. Non-smokers in those countries must be constantly aware of the relation between smoking and bad smells: *rooken/rieken* and *rauchen/riechen*. 'Wreak' means to inflict pain, hurt or injure, which smokers might ponder as they inflict their reeking smoke on others.

103 REFUTE/DENY A protagonist in an argument or quarrel may 'rebut', 'rebuff' or 'deny' his opponent's allegations, but he 'refutes' them only if he can show or prove that what they say is wrong. In other words, you can deny what a person said simply by saying, 'I deny what you say is true', but to refute his argument calls for facts in your support.

104 REPELLENT/REPELLANT The dictionaries are unhelpful about this. But I feel – perhaps more by instinct than science – that '-ent' is the adjective, '-ant' the substance which repels.

105 RESTAURATEUR Not 'restauranteur'. The keeper of a restaurant provides a 'restorative'. There is no such word as 'restorantive', hence no 'restauranteur'. Even writers and broadcasters about food make this mistake.

106 RESTIVE/RESTFUL Both words come from the same Latin origin: *restare*, to stay back. A 'restive' donkey is one which stubbornly refuses to move; and a 'restive' child, one who is constantly fidgeting. Neither suggests restfulness.

107 REVUE/REVIEW The one is light entertainment with music, the other another look at something.

108 RITES/RIGHTS 'Rites' are ceremonies; 'rights', what we all demand. The confusion is a favourite source of headline puns.

109 ROWING/ROWING Rowing (to rhyme with 'going') means to propel a boat on the water with oars. Rowing (to rhyme with 'ploughing') is a needless neologism for quarrelling. 'I asked them whether they rowed a lot', wrote a man who had interviewed a couple who had rowed across the Atlantic.

110 SATIRE/SATYR Latin *satira*, 'a discursive composition in verse treating of a variety of subjects; in classical use a poem in which prevalent follies or vices are assailed with ridicule or with serious denunciation'. Satyrs (L. *satyri*) were gods of classical mythology with the face and upper part of the body human and the lower parts animal – and some pretty beastly habits to match.

111 SEASONABLE/SEASONAL The two words are not interchangeable. You may have 'seasonal' unemployment among seaside deck-chair attendants at Christmas – but it is also the time when holly, mistletoe and mince-pies are 'seasonable'.

112 SIEGE/'SEIGE' Writers and typesetters seem to have given up as to whether it is 'i' before 'e' or 'e' before 'i', and now apparently trust to luck.

113 SMACK/SMATTER Something that 'smacks' has a taste, smell or a suggestion of whatever it may be compared with, from German *Geschmack*, taste. A 'smatter' or 'smattering' is a superficial knowledge.

114 SNARL-UPS, TAILBACKS AND GRIDLOCKS 'Snarling' has had two meanings since the Middle Ages: the noise made by a fierce animal (or even an angry person) and the twisting and tangling of hair, yarn, etc. To speak of traffic being 'snarled up', and the resulting 'snarl-up' (with or without hyphen), is therefore an example of an old word usefully revived – a kind of born-again archaism. 'Tailbacks' and 'gridlocks' are the result of such 'snarl-ups': the 'tailback' being a useful new word for a traffic queue (and what is 'queue' but the French word for tail?), whereas the 'gridlock' is a snarled-up road or street intersection. It comes from America, where city streets are often laid out in regular, grid-like patterns.

115 SOMNOLENT/SOMNOLESCENT/SOMNAMBULANT *Somnus* is Latin for sleep, *somnolentus*, for sleepy; and the '-escent' suffix denotes an inclination towards, or increase of, a state – as in pubescent girls, who get bigger every day. *Ambulare* is Latin for walking (in spite of the fact that an ambulance is now a vehicle for people unable to walk*) – so a somnambulant is a sleepwalker, who would find it difficult if not impossible to walk in a recumbent posture.

116 SPADE/SPAYED Cats are 'spayed', i.e. neutered; 'spade', apart from the implement used for digging, is also one of many offensive names for a Negro, from 'black as a spade', i.e. the card suit.

117 STRAIGHTENED/STRAITENED The middle English word *strecchen*, to stretch, brought about the adjectival word *stregt*, or *stragt*, meaning fully extended, not crooked, straight. It is not connected with

*The confusion comes from the adoption of a French term, *hôpital ambulant*, a 'walking', i.e. mobile, hospital. Like many others, this is a wartime annexation, because Britain's favourite enemy spoke French.

'strait', which comes from the Latin *strictus*, from *stringere*, to tighten, bind tightly (cf. 'string'). Thus to be 'in straitened circumstances' means that one is constricted, not stretched; and when in a straitjacket one is tied up, not kept erect.

118 STYLISH/STYLISTIC The first praises good style, the second classifies in a non-committal manner.

119 SUMMONED/SUMMONSED To be 'summoned' is to be called (together) for a meeting: one who is 'summonsed' is issued with a summons, or called by authority to attend a court hearing or some such legal proceedings. The archaic spelling *summonds* could well be revived for the second sense to avoid confusion.

120 TAKING SILK Contrary to the belief of some journalistic innocents, taking silk is not the same as stealing it. It is lawyers' jargon for the process by which a barrister becomes a Queen's Counsel, or QC (KC when there is a king on the throne). Lawyers thus honoured are colloquially described as 'silks', as in 'he was a distinguished silk'. The term comes from the silken gown worn by QCs and dates from about 1880.

121 THERMAL/WARM Not so much a malapropism as a tautology or, at best, a stilted euphemism for 'warm'. The recent fashion for 'thermal' has probably been brought about by firms which advertise 'thermal underwear' as though it were some kind of new scientific invention. 'Thermal' comes from the Greek word *thermos* = heat, which is also enshrined in the trade name of a vacuum flask which keeps things hot – or cold.

122 TOTING/TOUTING 'Toting' is an old American colloquialism meaning to carry a load or object, hence 'toting a gun'. 'Touting' means to look out importunately and eagerly for customers or employment – originally a word for peeping, peering or keeping a sharp lookout, hence the sense of searching for possible customers who might be willing to avail themselves of, say, a prostitute's service. By the curious conventions of that trade, men 'tout' and women 'solicit'. The cuttings shown fail to make clear whether the Beirut Arabs were wielding their machine-guns with a view to selling or firing them.

123 TROOPER/TROUPER A 'trooper' is a soldier. Actors and actresses (especially older ones and members of a troupe) are 'troupers'.

124 UNLOADED/UNLADEN An 'unladen' ship carries no cargo and is therefore not capable of being 'unloaded'. The illustration comes from a surprising source: Virginia Woolf's essay *The Docks of London*.

125 WAS/WERE

'Contrariwise', continued Tweedledee, 'if it was so, it might be; and if it were so, it would be: but as it ain't, it ain't. That's logic.'

Lewis Carroll, *Through the Looking-Glass*

Such subtleties find no place in the media today, for the present conditional 'were' is gradually being ousted by the colloquial 'was'. In my first term at an English public school the headmaster (an ordained priest) set an essay with the title 'If I was King'. I was rash enough to put my hand up and say. 'Please, sir, shouldn't we write, "If I were King"?' – for after all, I had only just been taught about the English conditional (though not at his school). I received six strokes: one, I reflected later, for impertinence and five for being right. If Shakespeare had been taught English by that headmaster he would have had *Macbeth* say, 'If it was done, when 'tis done, then 'twould be well if it was done quickly . . .' And the 'would be' for the second 'were' is borne out in the Good News Bible (1966): where the Authorised and Revised versions have 'were it not that I regard the presence of . . . the king . . . I would not look upon thee,' the GNB, while not stooping to 'was it not', has the crude compromise 'if I didn't respect'. It would be sad if the proper usage *were* to be lost.

126 WHILE/WILE 'While': to occupy and engage a person for a time, or to fill up the time. 'Wile': craftiness, cunning, deceit, etc.

127 WHISKEY/WHISKY The Scots were probably the first to distil this liquor, whose name comes from the Gaelic *uisgebeatha* (*uisge bheatha* or *usquebaugh* – authorities differ), meaning 'water of life'. But the Irish also have the drink, and call it 'whiskey', to distinguish it from the Scotch 'whisky' (colloquially simply 'Scotch') without the 'e'. 'Water of life' is a strange choice for a name when one considers that a whole bottle drunk at a single draught will give most people fatal alcoholic poisoning. Ancient alchemists called any unrectified alcohol they distilled *aqua vitae*, and various continental liquors go under the name of *Aquavit*.

128 WHO/WHOM If John Donne had lived and worked in twentieth-century Fleet Street he might have written: 'Ask not for who the bell tolls; it tolls for yourself'; and, conversely: 'Whomever loves, if he do not propose/The right true end of love, he's one that goes/To sea for nothing but to make him sick.' Part of the trouble lies in the difference between informal, chatty writing or speech (in which 'who d'you think you're fooling?' is not only acceptable but to be preferred to 'whom do you think you are fooling?') and formal, grammatical writing. And there is the added complication that writers who lack confidence about their cases choose 'whom' because they think it sounds more polite.

Corrections and Apologies

Everyone makes mistakes, and this book will be no exception. One or two blank pages have therefore been set aside at the end for readers to add their own corrections, amendments or additions. Yes, to err is human, but in this respect the daily press is more human than most of us. It is an old saying that 'whenever one reads anything about oneself in the papers they always get something wrong – starting usually with one's name'. Most such mistakes are trivial ('well, you know what we meant' is the standard explanation), but a frequent complaint is that errors of fact are seldom corrected or retracted in subsequent issues. Some politicians and trades-unionists, envious perhaps of foreign, state-controlled party-organs, have proposed legislation ranging from outright nationalisation to compulsory publication of corrections. Such an absurd and impractical scheme in a free country would provide wonderful opportunities for printing studied insults of the kind poor, pompous Mr Pooter was subjected to in the Grossmiths' *Diary of a Nobody*. Pooter complained that the *Blackfriars Bi-weekly News* had omitted his and his wife's name from a list of guests at the Mansion House ('May 9. Wrote to the *Blackfriars Bi-weekly News*, pointing out their omission'). The omission is rectified but in the correction the paper misprints the Pooters' name as 'Mr and Mrs C. Porter' (May 12. Wrote again and I took particular care to write out our name in capital letters, POOTER, so that there should be no possible mistake this time'). On 16 May, Mr Pooter is 'absolutely disgusted' to read: 'We have received two letters from Mr and Mrs Charles Pewter, requesting us to announce the important fact that they were at the Mansion House Ball' ('I tore up the paper and threw it in the wastepaper basket. My time is far too valuable to bother about such trifles').

This is on the lines of the old story about the colonel who had been inadvertently described as 'bottle-scarred'. He received an apology and a 'correction' – to 'battle-scared'. For there is no guarantee that the corrections themselves will be free from mistake. A *Guardian* reader recently complained in a letter that he was unable to complete a crossword because the six-letter clue led to the non-existent word 'fuggot' instead of 'faggot'. The printed 'correction' made it 'faggott'.

The Times, it should be said, does make a practice of publishing corrections, even those of a trivial nature, for it is a Newspaper of Record; and it must also be added in mitigation that telephone mishearings account for many a delightful mis-transcription.

A CORRECTION

IN A CAPTION in last night's *Evening Gazette*, Miss Dorothy Duffney, conductor of the Cleveland Musical Society, was described as Mrs Vera Beedle. She is, of course, Mrs K. Atkinson, of Hartburn Lane, Stock-

---

An Advertisement in the Evening Chronicle of 19th September, 1972, carried the sentence "Pot in the Park" — This should have read "Pop in the Park." We apologise to the Ton

---

MR ARTHUR RUBBRA

In Saturday's obituary of Mr Arthur Rubbra he was inadvertently referred to as Sir Arthur Rubbra.

IN yesterday's leader the name of Anthony Burgess should of course have read, Anthony Blunt. We apologise to readers for the error.

On Page 39 of today's Colour Magazine there is a reference to Nigel Burgess and his brother Anthony, "the spy". We should of course have referred to Guy Burgess. We apologise to Anthony Burgess, the distinguished author, for this mistake.

PS: Instructions for last fortnight's fresh lemon cake read three teaspoons of salt instead of half a teaspoon. Apologies to anyone who found it too salty.

IN the Manweb supplement on Tuesday, Cook up a taste of 1883! the ingredient of white fat in the pastry recipe for Perfect Apple Pie should have read 1oz and not 10oz as stated.

We apologise to Roger Pincham, Chairman of the Liberal Party, for a "not" that was misprinted as a "now" in the seventh paragraph of his letter of April 7. The clause concerned should have read "... but (the Falkland Islanders) must not be expected to face the total destruction of their community ..."

Correction

The photograph on April 21 of the Duchess of Gloucester's visit to the Aleck Bourne maternity unit at St Mary's Hospital, Paddington, should have referred to the Elm unit, not the Elm unit.

In this column last Friday, ing the BBC's Borgias, that The "I thought the snow just was made to observe, concern-as bad as the critics had said." The misprinting of "snow" for "show" was obviously caused by the adverse weather conditions prevailing

---

CORRECTION

A caricature of Mr Norman Willis, deputy general secretary of the TUC, was incorrectly described yesterday as being of Mr Alan Sapper.

In our recipe for Banana Trifle last week we inadvertently omitted the bananas. We apologise a

---

Correction

In the penultimate paragraph of the Whitehall brief article yesterday the word "for" was inadvertently omitted from the following sentence: "The safeguard is the media members of the committee, who are very sharp and fight for the press.

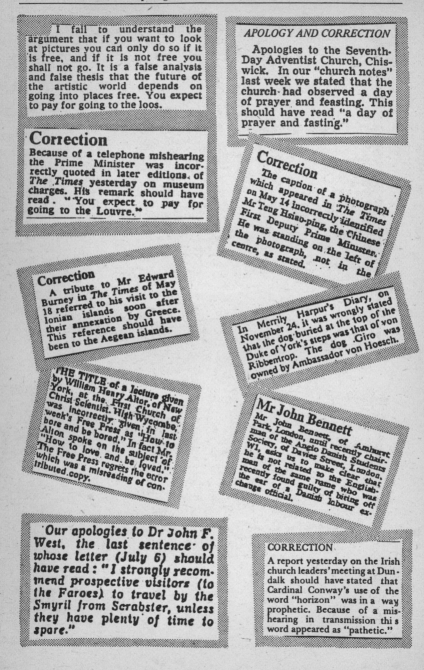

I fail to understand the argument that if you want to look at pictures you can only do so if it is free, and if it is not free you shall not go. It is a false analysis and false thesis that the future of the artistic world depends on going into places free. You expect to pay for going to the loos.

Correction

Because of a telephone mishearing the Prime Minister was incorrectly quoted in later editions of The Times yesterday on museum charges. His remark should have read. "You expect to pay for going to the Louvre."

Correction

A tribute to Mr Edward Burney in The Times of May 18 referred to his visit to the Ionian islands soon after their annexation by Greece. This reference should have been to the Aegean islands.

THE TITLE of a lecture given by William Henry Altor, of New York, at the First Church of Christ Scientist, High Wycombe, was incorrectly given in last week's Free Press as "How to bore and be bored." In fact Mr Alton spoke on the subject of "How to love and be loved." The Free Press regrets the error which was a misreading of contributed copy.

Our apologies to Dr John F. West, the last sentence of whose letter (July 6) should have read: "I strongly recommend prospective visitors (to the Faroes) to travel by the Smyril from Scrabster, unless they have plenty of time to spare."

APOLOGY AND CORRECTION

Apologies to the Seventh-Day Adventist Church, Chiswick. In our "church notes" last week we stated that the church had observed a day of prayer and feasting. This should have read "a day of prayer and fasting."

Correction

The caption of a photograph which appeared in The Times on May 14 incorrectly identified Mr Teng Hsiao-ping, the Chinese First Deputy Prime Minister. He was standing on the left of the photograph, not in the centre, as stated.

In Merrily Harpur's Diary, on November 24, it was wrongly stated that the dog buried at the top of the Duke of York's steps was that of von Ribbentrop. The dog Giro was owned by Ambassador von Hoesch.

Mr John Bennett

Mr John Bennett, of Amhurst Park, London, until recently chairman of the Anglo Danish Students Society, of Davies Street, London, W1, asks us to make clear that he is not related to the English-man of the same name who was recently found guilty of biting off the ear of a Danish labour exchange official.

CORRECTION

A report yesterday on the Irish church leaders' meeting at Dundalk should have stated that Cardinal Conway's use of the word "horizon" was in a way prophetic. Because of a mishearing in transmission this word appeared as "pathetic."

Correction

Last week, we described the new Convenor of the teacher education sector of the London Students' Organisation, Val Furness, as "a Communist Party candidate." She feels this description is ambiguous and needs to be clarified. She is a member of the Communist Party of Britain (Marxist-Leninist). She is not a member of the Communist Party of England (Marxist-Leninist), or the Communist Party of Great Britain, the Communist League, or the Communist Federation of Britain (Marxist-Leninist). She would like to say that she is not in the Broad Left either.

Due to a misunderstanding over the telephone we stated that the couple would live at the home of the bridegroom's father.

We have been asked to point out that they will in fact live at The Old Manse.

We regret that owing to a typographical error the closing sentence of Sir David Llewellyn's article yesterday appeared as "Blessed are the merciful, for they shall receive money." "Money" should have read "mercy."

The word "unfortunate" in the letter from Lord Wedderburn of Charlton yesterday should have been "fortunate".

Israel weighs the risks: In a Leader on June 17 the reference to "Mr Begin's plan" was a mishearing for Mr Reagan's plan.—Ed., Gdn

Correction

Shaikh Muhammad al-Fassi is not a nephew of King Fahd of Saudi Arabia, as stated on July 14. He is related to the king by the marriage of his sister to Prince Turki.

Mr. Stephen Boulding, whose name was inadvertently misspelt in last week's report of the Young Conservatives' conference at Eastbourne, asks us to state that the phrase he used in his speech in a harmless, mock-serious vein was "Frogs and Italians". Owing to an error in transmission this was reported as "wogs and Italians".

Correction

The caption to an item headed "New bishop enthroned" on September 22 incorrectly stated that the Bishop of London, Dr Graham. Leonard, had performed the traditional ceremony of knocking on the main door of St Paul's Cathedral. The ceremony had been deleted from the order of service by the Dean and Chapter, and the main door was opened in advance of the bishop's arrival, as a gesture of welcome.

Correction

The omission of a sentence from Frank Johnson's column on May 12 made it appear incorrectly that the Speaker had declined to take a point of order from Mr Andrew Faulds in the previous day's proceedings in the House of Commons.

CORRECTIONS AND AMENDMENTS

CORRECTIONS AND AMENDMENTS

CORRECTIONS AND AMENDMENTS

CORRECTIONS AND AMENDMENTS

Fritz Spiegl
Dead Funny £1.50

'Beneath this sod lies another' – the long-awaited sequel to *A Small Book of Grave Humour* from the ever-watchful Spiegl who, during the years of success of his first collection of the funnier side of tombstones, has continued to collect mirthful *mementos mori*. He has now put together a second book which promises to be every bit as popular as the first.

A Small Book of Grave Humour £1.50

'The object of an epitaph is to identify the resting place of the mortal remains of a dead person. It should therefore record only such information as is reasonably necessary for that purpose' – *Churchyard Handbook*. Thank heaven the above injunction has not always been strictly observed – as witness the following examples from this touching, very funny collection:

'Here lies Lester Moore . . . Four slugs from a 44 . . . No less no more.'

'Here lieth Mary, the wife of John Ford . . . We hope her soul is gone to the Lord . . . But if for Hell she has changed this life, she had better be there than be John Ford's wife.'

Bernard Levin
Speaking Up £2.50

more of the best of his journalism

'The nearest thing to a national institution of any journalist who has emerged in this country since the war' CHRISTOPHER BOOKER

'A welcome selection of the works of Scoop Levin, the ace reporter . . . and a dozen other Levin personae . . . the sharpest, funniest, saddest columnist of our generation' THE TIMES

'Characteristically provocative, brilliant and readable' YORKSHIRE POST

'The most remarkable journalist of our time' PHILIP TOYNBEE

Denys Parsons
The Best of Shrdlu £1

The irrepressible Shrdlu is that malicious spirit who lurks at the elbow of weary printers and journalists to produce such disastrous printed consequences as:

'Thieves stole 600 loaves of bread from an empty delivery van yesterday.'

'For sale: Lovely rosewood piano. Owner going abroad with beautiful twisted legs.'

'Ghana is to change over to driving on the right. The change will be made gradually.'

Here is the cream of Shrdlology, culled from the best-selling *Funny* series, and accompanied by many brand-new gems.

Jim Douglas
How to Live with a Working Wife £1.95

If she's out at work, then it's down to you, brother. When the washing machine goes ape, when the kids acquire strange infestations, when all your careful planning dissolves into a domestic holocaust . . . That's when you need this little book of expertise, wisdom and cheerful advice. A man who can iron a shirt with only five expert strokes can do anything. Who needs a woman's touch when you can put your great big masculine foot in it?

Viv Quillan
Taking the Lid off Kids £1.50

What starts as a twinkle in father's eye, becomes an expected happy event, and ends up as *a kid*. Kids. They are all here, from the Accumulator who hoards secondhand chewing gum and dead birds, to the Zombie, comatose in front of the television, emerging only to check for spots and split ends. An A-Z of kids, guaranteed non-fiction.

Christopher Ward
Our Cheque is in the Post £1.50

A book of excuses from the author of *How to Complain*.

'Reasons for not helping with the washing up . . . being late, leaving early; excuses for being drunk . . . avoiding dancing or sex; convincing things to tell policemen and what to do if you are caught out telling a lie'
DAILY TELEGRAPH

'Very useful some of these tips are. Reason you didn't telephone when you promised you would: one of the children snipped through the cable with wire clippers' KEITH WATERHOUSE, DAILY MIRROR

Rob Buckman
Jogging From Memory £1.25

Hangovers, insomnia, Sunday papers, Heidegger, hi-fi, Round Britain Quizzes and why Ibsen's plays are really comic masterpieces – just some of the topics dealth with by broadcasting's funniest doctor. Thirty enlightening and hilarious essays from one of today's foremost humourists, enhanced by the brilliant cartoons of Martin Honeysett and concluding with an introduction from Dr Sigmund Freud (deceased).

'If you don't bust a gut with laughter, you can sue me' DR SIGMUND FREUD

Out of Practice 95p

Do you need a course of yellow fever injections to enter a Chinese restaurant? Did your father ever strip naked, do handsprings against the bathroom door while shrieking out French irregular verbs? No? Between the covers of this book lurk the innermost thoughts and crazy experiences of a practising medic – the only man to invent a cure for which there is no known disease. Illustrated by Bill Tidy, this hilarious book's author is still a practising registrar in a London hospital.

'The funniest thing to come out of a hospital since Richard Gordon'
SHERIDAN MORLEY

Ronnie Barker
Fletcher's Book of Rhyming Slang £1.25

Get the brass tacks on what come out of the old north and south. 'Everybody has heard of rhyming slang. It dates back to time immoral. At least a hundred and fifty years, because the wife's mother doesn't remember it starting . . .' – says Ronnie Barker. He's put together a hilarious dictionary and phrase book of Cockney rhyming slang, ancient and modern, exactly as she is spoke. Take a butcher's!

Robert Morley
illustrated by Geoffrey Dickinson and John Jensen
Robert Morley's Book of Bricks £1.50

The hilarious, bestselling collection of things people say – and then wish they hadn't . . .

'Whatever happened to that skinny blonde your husband was once married to?'
'I dyed my hair,' replied the lady.

A whole concert of clangers culled from everyone who will admit to brick-dropping.

All royalties donated to the National Society for Autistic Children.

Robert Morley's Book of Worries £1.50

Do you have sleepless nights worrying about money, sex, age, diet, cars – even being buried alive or having an aeroplane fall on you? You do? Then take heart, for there is at least one other person like you – Robert Morley to be exact. Increase your anxiety potential with this hilarious guide to worrying peppered with that magic only the master himself can produce.

Nicholas Parsons
Dipped in Vitriol £1.75

'Perception of badness, as of beauty, is in the eye of the beholder . . . This is a humorous excursion through the realms of badness, highlighting self-importance in autobiography, pretentiousness and incompetence in fiction, mountebankery and shallowness in theatre, whimsical follies in music, brain-crushing false goods in cinema . . .'

A hilarious survey of hatchet reviews of the arts through the epochs – vitriolic offerings from Clive James, Bernard Levin, Gore Vidal, Oscar Wilde, Richard Ingrams, the *Sun*, *Pravda*, George Bernard Shaw and many more.

Simon Hoggart
On the House £1.50

Merry tales from the Mother of Parliaments by Westminster's wickedest columnist . . . Sir Keith Joseph pursued by a punk of dissenting views; George Brown inviting the papal nuncio to dance; the surprising video-viewing habits of Tony Benn; plus everything you always wanted to know about Nott, the defence minister   . the finest wit and wisdom from the celebrated *Punch* column.

'Some of his tales are incredible, but most are hilariously plausible. Even if Mr Hoggart's stories are not true, they should be' OBSERVER

Simon Hoggart
Back on the House £1.50

More merriment from the Mother of Parliaments by the celebrated *Punch* columnist. While PM Thatcher leads the nation to military triumph in a far-flung ocean, her husband is reincarnated in a popular theatrical entertainment, and the Social Democrats give a new meaning to the ancient tradition of the card vote – Access and Barclaycard accepted – to break the mould of political life. A second collection of wit and wickedness from the author of *On the House*.

Fiction

☐	**Options**	Freda Bright	£1.50p
☐	**The Thirty-nine Steps**	John Buchan	£1.50p
☐	**Secret of Blackoaks**	Ashley Carter	£1.50p
☐	**Hercule Poirot's Christmas**	Agatha Christie	£1.25p
☐	**Dupe**	Liza Cody	£1.25p
☐	**Lovers and Gamblers**	Jackie Collins	£2.50p
☐	**Sphinx**	Robin Cook	£1.25p
☐	**Ragtime**	E. L. Doctorow	£1.50p
☐	**My Cousin Rachel**	Daphne du Maurier	£1.95p
☐	**Mr American**	George Macdonald Fraser	£2.25p
☐	**The Moneychangers**	Arthur Hailey	£2.25p
☐	**Secrets**	Unity Hall	£1.75p
☐	**Black Sheep**	Georgette Heyer	£1.75p
☐	**The Eagle Has Landed**	Jack Higgins	£1.95p
☐	**Sins of the Fathers**	Susan Howatch	£2.95p
☐	**The Master Sniper**	Stephen Hunter	£1.50p
☐	**Smiley's People**	John le Carré	£1.95p
☐	**To Kill a Mockingbird**	Harper Lee	£1.95p
☐	**Ghosts**	Ed McBain	£1.75p
☐	**Gone with the Wind**	Margaret Mitchell	£3.50p
☐	**Blood Oath**	David Morrell	£1.75p
☐	**Platinum Logic**	Tony Parsons	£1.75p
☐	**Wilt**	Tom Sharpe	£1.75p
☐	**Rage of Angels**	Sidney Sheldon	£1.95p
☐	**The Unborn**	David Shobin	£1.50p
☐	**A Town Like Alice**	Nevile Shute	£1.75p
☐	**A Falcon Flies**	Wilbur Smith	£1.95p
☐	**The Deep Well at Noon**	Jessica Stirling	£1.95p
☐	**The Ironmaster**	Jean Stubbs	£1.75p
☐	**The Music Makers**	E. V. Thompson	£1.95p

Non-fiction

☐	**Extraterrestrial Civilizations**	Isaac Asimov	£1.50p
☐	**Pregnancy**	Gordon Bourne	£2.95p
☐	**Jogging From Memory**	Rob Buckman	£1.25p
☐	**The 35mm Photographer's Handbook**	Julian Calder and John Garrett	£5.95p
☐	**Travellers' Britain**	Arthur Eperon	£2.95p
☐	**Travellers' Italy**		£2.50p
☐	**The Complete Calorie Counter**	Eileen Fowler	75p

☐	**The Diary of Anne Frank**	Anne Frank	£1.75p
☐	**And the Walls Came Tumbling Down**	Jack Fishman	£1.95p
☐	**Linda Goodman's Sun Signs**	Linda Goodman	£2.50p
☐	**Dead Funny**	Fritz Spiegl	£1.50p
☐	**How to be a Gifted Parent**	David Lewis	£1.95p
☐	**Victoria RI**	Elizabeth Longford	£4.95p
☐	**Symptoms**	Sigmund Stephen Miller	£2.50p
☐	**Book of Worries**	Robert Morley	£1.50p
☐	**Airport International**	Brian Moynahan	£1.75p
☐	**The Alternative Holiday Catalogue**	edited by Harriet Peacock	£1.95p
☐	**The Pan Book of Card Games**	Hubert Phillips	£1.75p
☐	**Food for All the Family**	Magnus Pyke	£1.50p
☐	**Just Off for the Weekend**	John Slater	£2.50p
☐	**An Unfinished History of the World**	Hugh Thomas	£3.95p
☐	**The Baby and Child Book**	Penny and Andrew Stanway	£4.95p
☐	**The Third Wave**	Alvin Toffler	£2.75p
☐	**Pauper's Paris**	Miles Turner	£2.50p
☐	**The Flier's Handbook**		£5.95p

All these books are available at your local bookshop or newsagent, or can be ordered direct from the publisher. Indicate the number of copies required and fill in the form below   9

....

Name_____
(Block letters please)

Address_____

_____

Send to Pan Books (CS Department), Cavaye Place, London SW10 9PG
Please enclose remittance to the value of the cover price plus:
35p for the first book plus 15p per copy for each additional book ordered
to a maximum charge of £1.25 to cover postage and packing
Applicable only in the UK

While every effort is made to keep prices low, it is sometimes
necessary to increase prices at short notice. Pan Books reserve
the right to show on covers and charge new retail prices which
may differ from those advertised in the text or elsewhere